ELVIS: THE LOUISIANA HAYRIDE YEARS
1954 - 1956

Louisiana Hayride, Inc.
www.louisianahayrideinc.com
www.elvisatthehayride.com

ELVIS

THE Louisiana Hayride YEARS

1954 - 1956

by Frank Page with Joey Kent

Louisiana Hayride, Inc.

Managing Editor: Luigi Agostini
Research & Development: Joey Kent
Illustration: Kenny Durham
Photo Restoration and Collage: Joey Kent
Production & Creative Design: Susan Winship
Book Production: Jim Bacca
Book Design: Kira Evans
           based on an original layout by Joey Kent

Copyright © 2006
Louisiana Hayride, Inc.
14 Walsh Drive, Suite 102
Parsippany, NJ 07054-1101

LIBRARY OF CONGRESS NUMBER: 2006921421

ISBN-13: 978-0-9778305-1-0
ISBN-10:   0-9778305-1-9

90000>

9 780977 830510

Printed in Korea.

TABLE OF CONTENTS

ACKNOWLEDGEMENTS

"Thank ya. Thankyaverymuch."

Stories, photos and material
contributed by:

David Kent
Frank Page
Joey Kent
Horace Logan
Norm Bale
Bob Sullivan
Tillman Franks
Joyce Railsback Nichols
Tom Bevins
Maxine Brown
Bonnie Brown
Jim Ed Brown
Gary Bryant
Billy Walker
Jeanette Hicks
Betty Amos
Tom Perryman
Ronnie McDowell
Vera "Dido" Rowley
Slim Whitman
Jimmy Lee Fautheree
Stan Lewis
Ginny Wright
Langston McEachern

Jack Barham
Lloyd Stilley
J. Frank McAneny
Eric J. Brock
Marie Graham Gadpaille
Trish Lutz
Karl & Judy Heiserman
Ernst Jorgensen
Robert Gentry
Carol Mangham
Gail Reaben
Ann Paulsen
Lois Ann Rivers
Raye Lynn Wiley
Joe Johnson
Robert Hassell Fair
Nolan Strange
Robert Catts
Wayne Everett
Lamar Baker
the LSU-S Archives
the Henry Clay family
Tom Pace
Johnny Wessler

and many others...

DEDICATIONS

To my wife, Helen, and daughter, Patti, who are the most loving and caring people on earth.

To Henry Clay, Horace Logan, Dean Upson, Tillman Franks, and A.M. "Pappy" Covington who helped start and sustain the Louisiana Hayride.

To the hundreds of "wannabes" who didn't find success on the show.

To the announcers, engineers, producers, musicians, stage crew, KWKH staff, doormen, ticket sellers and takers, artists, their managers, concessionaires, groupies, and the audience.

To the Grand Ole Opry for turning Elvis down.

To Joey Kent who is the most talented writer, partner, finagler, computer guru and bird dog on the planet.

And of course, to Elvis who had the innate talent and looks and was in the right place at the right time.

- Frank Page

(CLOCKWISE FROM TOP LEFT)
JOEY & AMBER KENT, FRANK & HELEN PAGE,
JOEY KENT AND FRANK PAGE

To my father, David Kent, who carried on the Louisiana Hayride legacy and hoped one day I'd be a writer; to my mother, Loraine, who has financed more Hayride dreams than anyone will ever know; to my friend Frank and all the others who believe in me, especially my wife Amber who is my biggest cheerleader. Special thanks to Ernst Jorgensen for the use of his extensive photo collection, and to Elvis fans everywhere for deeming this publication worthy.   *- Joey Kent*

FOREWORD

In this day and age, it is popular to research one's roots. If you were a member of the Presley family, you would want to go to Tupelo where he was born, then to Memphis where he made his first recordings at Sun Studios. But if you wanted to know the defining moment when he came of age, spread his wings and began to fly... if you wanted to see "where it all began", then you'd travel to Shreveport, Louisiana and walk the halls of the Municipal Auditorium where Elvis honed his craft some fifty years ago on the stage of the Louisiana Hayride.

On October 16, 1954, a young, unpolished and even shy 19 year-old Presley walked out on the stage of the Louisiana Hayride and changed not only the face of our show, but the face of music forever. On a moment's notice, I was elected to orchestrate that incredible moment and introduce Elvis to radio listeners worldwide. Neither Elvis nor I knew how important his Hayride debut would become to so many people around the world, and there was no predicting his meteoric rise to stardom. We watched him go from earning less than $20 a week to $200 to $2000 and more in the short span of 18 months he was on our show.

In this book, Joey Kent and I have put together a collection of pictures and memories in an attempt to recapture the moments that turned the musical world around. Relive them with us as we journey back in time to a much more gentle era, where a slight movement of a leg was enough to gain censorship on the new medium of television. Times have indeed changed... and change is constant, so enjoy the moments. They won't be back.

Frank Page

Shreveport, Louisiana

* Louisiana Hayride *

WHERE IT ALL BEGAN

Dr. William Hunt shared the news with the congregation of the Second Baptist Church of Tupelo, Mississippi at their Wednesday prayer meeting. The day before, January 8, 1935, identical twin sons had been born to Vernon and Gladys Presley. Jesse Garon was stillborn. Elvis Aron survived.

Young Elvis spent an impoverished childhood in Tupelo. His mother took him regularly to church and this strict ritual coupled with his parent's love molded Elvis into a non-drinking, non-smoking, polite God-fearing young man. Bill Dugard, a former car salesman here in Shreveport and a good friend of mine, grew up in Tupelo, East Tupelo to be exact, lived next door to Elvis. They spent a lot of time together going to school and playing. Bill remembers a setting on the edge of town with trees on one side, their favorite swimming hole (a creek) on another side and bottom land to the north. They played "cowboys and Indians" with stick guns but their favorite fantasy was driving their make-believe cars. The top of a lard can served as the steering wheel for their foot-powered vehicles. Bill and Elvis drove the lands where no 4X4 could ever go, limited only by their imaginations.

Neither boy had a bicycle, wagon or BB gun but they did have sling shots or "bean shooters", as we called them back then. One day, Bill shot a rock into a bunch of sparrows killing one of them. Elvis cried and cried at the sight and couldn't understand how Bill could have killed a living thing. Elvis had a soft heart.

At age ten, Elvis won his first talent contest with a rendition of Red Foley's tear-jerker "Ol' Shep." In 1948, the year the Hayride started, the Presley family packed everything into a '39 Plymouth and moved to Memphis, Tennessee. Influenced by the big city, Elvis let his sideburns grow.

Elvis graduated high school when he was eighteen and, for a while, drove a delivery truck for the Crown Electric Company to

ELVIS' BOYHOOD HOME IN TUPELO.

earn a living. During the summer of 1953, he went into Sam Phillips' Sun Records studio to record a two sided acetate of "My Happiness" and "That's When Your Heartaches Begin" for his mother's approaching birthday. It cost Elvis all of four dollars. The following summer, on the recommendation of Phillips, Elvis was contacted by local guitarist Scotty Moore to audition for his band, "The Starlite Wranglers." Soon after, Scotty, Elvis, and bass player Bill

Black reported to Sun Studios for a rehearsal session where Sam eventually heard something he liked. The trio worked out six songs: "That's All Right, Mama", "Blue Moon Of Kentucky", "Good Rockin' Tonight", "I Don't Care (If The Sun Don't Shine)", "Milk Cow Blues Boogie", and "You're A Heartbreaker."

From then on, Elvis was the featured singer. Scotty and Bill were destined to be his first band and both would achieve lasting success in the music world.

990KC   1000 WATTS

Franklin Page

"Voice of the Tri-States"

KWEM

West Memphis, Arkansas

FRANK PAGE   MEMPHIS 8-0518
PROGRAM DIRECTOR   W. MEMPHIS 463

BUSINESS CARD OF YOUNG ANNOUNCER FRANK PAGE, JUST GETTING STARTED IN MEMPHIS TOO - **1947.**

ELVIS, SCOTTY & BILL THE NIGHT OF THEIR FIRST LOUISIANA HAYRIDE. SHOW ANNOUNCER FRANK PAGE LOOKS ON FROM THE SIDE - **OCTOBER 16, 1954.**

Elvis Presley was just nineteen years old and fresh from this first Sun Records recording session when he made his debut on the Louisiana Hayride in the fall of 1954. He came to us quiet and unsure. There was no snarl, no hip and leg gyrations. He was just starting out and it would be many more months before Elvis would fully understand what audiences needed from him and what he so desperately needed from them. He was there to learn, to grow... to find himself as an artist.

I had the pleasure of introducing Elvis to radio audiences worldwide that crisp, fall evening and saw first hand the raw, savage talent that would one day make him King of Rock 'N' Roll.

The setting was Shreveport, Louisiana, a medium-sized oil town on the banks of the Red River in northwest Louisiana just thirteen miles from the Texas line. My Employer, radio station KWKH, was in its seventh year of broadcasting the Louisiana Hayride. The Hayride was a three and a half hour country music program called by many "the junior Grand Ole Opry." This was no showcase of made talent; the Hayride was a place where acts were developed and stars were born. Nicknamed "the Cradle of the Stars," the Hayride by this time had already given rise to such popular country artists such as Hank Williams, Kitty Wells, the Wilburn Brothers, Webb Pierce, Slim Whitman, Red Sovine, Jim Reeves and many others. It is into this daunting field of country legends that a young "folk music" artist from Memphis, Tennessee tried to stake his own claim to fame that evening.

(ABOVE) HANK WILLIAMS AND THE HAYRIDE CAST - **NOVEMBER, 1948**. (TOP RIGHT) SHREVEPORT'S SPOTLIGHT MAGAZINE ANNOUNCES THE ARRIVAL OF THE HAYRIDE'S NEWEST STAR - **DECEMBER, 1954**.

DEDICATED IN 1929 AS A MEMORIAL TO THOSE LOST IN "THE GREAT WORLD WAR," SHREVEPORT'S 3800-SEAT MUNICIPAL AUDITORIUM WAS HOME TO THE LOUISIANA HAYRIDE FROM 1948 TO 1960.

Shreveport's Municipal Auditorium, an impressive 3800 seat facility located on the west side of downtown, was the home base for the Hayride. At the turn of the century, the surrounding neighborhood, known as St. Paul's Bottoms, was part of one of the largest legal red light districts in the country. Madam Annie McCune had the biggest house and the prettiest gals and on a Saturday night back then you'd likely find a little known blues man by the name of Leadbelly strumming his guitar from one of the porches as the ladies of the evening sashayed by on the arms of their gentlemen callers. Renamed Ledbetter Heights some years back in honor of the now famous blues man, the neighborhood today is a shadow of its former self; grandeur given way to decay and the push towards suburbia.

The date was October 16, 1954. Tickets for the Louisiana Hayride were sixty cents for general admission and one dollar for the reserve section. Children got in for half price. Cokes and popcorn were a nickel each. Twenty eight hundred and sixteen fans of country music, give or take a few, passed through the doors of the Municipal Auditorium that evening, little knowing their music, indeed their world was about to change forever.

Headlining the Hayride show was Oklahoma native Floyd Tillman, most famous perhaps for his hit "Slipping Around." The cast of regulars included Betty Amos, Buddy Attaway, Jack Ford, Jeanette Hicks, Hoot & Curley, and Martha Lawson.

The current heartthrob among the ladies was Tibby Edwards. A certified Cajun from South Louisiana, Tibby was quite the ladies man both on stage and

HUDDIE LEDBETTER AKA "LEADBELLY"

off. And speaking of South Louisiana, Jimmy C. Newman who hails from deep in the bayou country near Big Mamou was also on hand. Jimmy was enjoying chart success with "Cry, Cry, Darling," and to this day he's quick to tell you the "C" in his name stands for Cajun.

HAYRIDE STAR TIBBY EDWARDS

You'd find a fair mix of music on the show that night and every Saturday night. The Hayride was the first show of its kind to feature drums in the house band and was open to most any kind of instrumentation; from Jimmy C.'s native accordion or "squeezebox," to the Hawaiian twangs of Hoot's steel guitar. One year we even brought in the string section of the Shreveport Symphony to back Slim Whitman on "Rose Marie."

Each show contained a number of gospel tunes, an instrumental here and there and even a blues song or two; in addition to the traditional country songs and western ballads that gave country western music its name. You'd hear Texas swing one minute and rapid-fire bluegrass the next. Yodelers competed with square dance callers to raise the rafters long into the night. All in all, we had a little something for everyone. City folks called it all "hillbilly music" - backwoods "noise" played by barefoot moonshiners with toothless grins and straw hats. But we knew better.

On a typical Hayride Saturday night, there were almost as many people backstage as there were out front! Singers, fans, musicians, agents, managers, promoters, you name it. Folks wandered around backstage and in and out of the dressing rooms all night long. The Louisiana Hayride was their big Saturday night social event - a chance to mingle, trade guitar licks, see and be seen, and maybe even book a tour or ink a record deal. A search of the dressing rooms or coat pockets might even have turned up a flask or two of whiskey - but you didn't hear it from me.

The Hayride didn't have an Artist Services Bureau at that time but if you were looking for a booking agent, manager, talent scout, sideman, teacher, songwriter or just somebody to jam with,

you'd find them all in Tillman Franks. Tillman was a bass player for the Hayride and managed Webb Pierce, Slim Whitman, Johnny Horton, Jimmy & Johnny and others during their days on our show.

The producer of our show and chief emcee was Horace Logan. Horace often dressed the part of the "bad guy" in his all black cowboy outfit, but he had a big heart and helped a lot of folks up the ladder of success. Most Saturday nights, Horace could be seen sporting a matched set of pearl handle revolvers. In 1953, Webb Pierce had bet him folks would never buy what he termed "a silly song about a boy" that had recently been cut by one of our announcers. Well, Jim Reeves sold 600,000 copies of "Bimbo," and cost Webb a couple of fine firearms. Horace wore them every Saturday night thereafter.

Sam Phillips accompanied Elvis, Scotty and Bill on their trip down to Shreveport

CAJUN SENSATION JIMMY C. NEWMAN

HAYRIDE STAR WEBB PIERCE

one had something special about it. Neither Elvis nor these two songs really fit the Hayride or the country music pattern of the time, but it was the consensus of our group to give the kid a shot.

Horace usually introduced the main attractions on the Hayride but since Elvis was an unknown, I was asked to do the honors. When Elvis first came out and started singing, he sorta rocked forward on his feet and looked like he was about to leap right out into the audience. He shook his legs just a bit but I believe that

and looked on from the fourth row as his artist was introduced. It hadn't been two weeks since Sam first called the Hayride to ask if he could secure a spot for his new act. Elvis had just finished a run playing the Grand Ole Opry and, while the audience seemed to enjoy his performance, the talent manager Jim Denny told Elvis he might oughta stick to driving a truck. This discouraged the teenager and Sam knew he had to do something to get the momentum building again. He spoke first with Tillman who referred him over to Pappy Covington. Pappy was the building manager for the auditorium and acted as a talent booker for the show. Together they approached Horace and me.

Local disc jockey T. Tommy Cutrer had been playing Elvis' 45 around town, mostly as a favor to his old buddy Sam, and folks assumed Elvis was some new black artist. The "A" side featured "That's All Right, Mama," a blues song that was cut about 15 years earlier by Arthur "Big Boy" Crudup, and the flip side was a bluesy rendition of Bill Monroe's "Blue Moon Of Kentucky."

As far as recordings go, we'd heard a lot better and certainly a lot worse but this

LOUISIANA HAYRIDE PROGRAM DIRECTOR
AND CHIEF EMCEE HORACE LOGAN

SHREVEPORT DISC JOCKEY
T. TOMMY CUTRER

Too Young To Die." With each passing country favorite, though, the audience found they were unable to shake the memory of what they just witnessed, unable to deny the energy that spread like a virus among them.

HAYRIDE STAFF FIDDLER
DOBBER JOHNSON

As each act concluded, they chanted for the return of the folk artist with the peculiar magnetism and began to shift in their seats and grumble when he failed to reappear. The acts they'd come to know as family now seemed distant and boring. Slowly, they built their enthusiasm for the young trio from Memphis and when Elvis, Scotty, and Bill were called back out later in the show, the reception was very different.

The talk had begun and even though Elvis repeated the same two songs, he was more relaxed... more in tune with the pleasure of the audience. The result

was nerves more than anything else. All in all, I'd say he showed restraint before the crowd of mostly older, married couples. He seemed at times pinned in, like he was struggling to contain this enormous kinetic force. It slipped out a little there at the end and, to my surprise, the audience seemed to connect with and even appreciate what Elvis was doing. His two upbeat and bluesy songs were down right in the middle of a run of classic country; Ginny Wright's rather demure rendition of "Tell Me How To Get Married" on one end and Dobber Johnson's "splinter-bustin" hoedown, "Black Mountain Rag" on the other. That, more so perhaps than his pink getup, made Elvis stand out all the more.

The rest of the evening wasn't much different, I'm afraid. Hoot & Curley followed Dobber with, "Battered Old Raincoat," then Tibby came out and put his spin on Ray Price's recent hit "Much

HAYRIDE STAR GINNY WRIGHT

ELVIS CASTS A WARY EYE AT GRAND OLE OPRY TALENT MANAGER JIM DENNY. THE LOUISIANA HAYRIDE HAD AN INTENSE RIVALRY WITH THE TENNESSEE BASED OPRY, OFTEN REFERRING TO THE SHOW ON THE AIR AS "HAYRIDE EAST."

garnered him an invitation to return and a spot as a regular on the Louisiana Hayride.

November the sixth marked Elvis' first show as a regular of the Louisiana Hayride, joining an all-star cast that included Jim Reeves, Slim Whitman, Johnny Horton, Jimmy C. Newman, and the Browns. In the three weeks since his first Hayride performance, word had spread that this hillbilly cat was really something to see, and Elvis had no trouble earning encores. With just two singles to their credit, the trio filled out the performance with covers of "I'm Gonna Sit Right Down And Cry", "Fool, Fool, Fool", and "Sittin' On Top Of The World."

As the clear channel signal of KWKH swept the southwest and beamed the radio program into millions of homes, Elvis caught the attention of young people everywhere. Joyce Railsback was a teenager growing up in the west Texas town of Big Spring, some 500 miles from Shreveport. Every Saturday night she would tune in the Hayride and listen to the show until her parents called "lights out." Even then, a flashlight would keep her writing down the details of the program in her journal well past bedtime.

When Elvis sang "Fool, Fool, Fool" that evening, she wrote "he has a strange and different style and may go places with it." Truer words were never spoken.

JOYCE RAILSBACK

JOYCE RAILSBACK'S DIARY FOR
NOVEMBER 6, 1954

(CLOCKWISE FROM TOP LEFT) HAYRIDE REGULARS HOOT & CURLEY; HAYRIDE ANNOUNCERS FRANK PAGE, NORM BALE AND HORACE LOGAN; FRANK PAGE BRINGS ON THE NEXT ACT; FRANK PAGE; ELVIS HIDING OUT BETWEEN SETS; FRANK PAGE.

Elvis' First Contract with the Hayride

STATE OF LOUISIANA :

PARISH OF CADDO :

      THIS AGREEMENT ENTERED INTO BY AND BETWEEN INTERNATIONAL BROADCASTING CORPORATION, A LOUISIANA CORPORATION, LICENSEE AND OPERATOR OF RADIO STATION KWKH, HEREINAFTER SOMETIMES REFERRED TO AS STATION, REPRESENTED BY   H. L. Logan

_____ ,

AND

Elvis Presley, William Black and Winfred Scott ,

HEREINAFTER SOMETIMES REFERRED TO AS ARTIST:

W I T N E S S E T H:

1.

      STATION OPERATES A 50,000 WATT RADIO STATION IN SHREVEPORT, LOUISIANA, AND IN CONJUNCTION THEREWITH RENDERS CERTAIN MUSICAL PROGRAMS OVER THE AIR AND CONDUCTS A PERFORMANCE KNOWN AS THE "LOUISIANA HAYRIDE" BOTH ON THE AIR AND AS A PUBLIC PERFORMANCE WITH AUDIENCE, AND OTHERWISE EMPLOYS MUSICIANS AND MUSICAL PERSONNEL IN ITS ACTIVITIES.

2.

      ARTIST IS A MUSICIAN AND SINGER AND IS INTERESTED IN HAVING HIS TALENTS PUBLICIZED THROUGH THE CHANNELS AVAILABLE TO STATION.

3.

      BEGINNING SATURDAY, 6 November 1954 , AND CONTINUING FOR FIFTY-TWO (52) CONSECUTIVE SATURDAYS THEREAFTER, ARTIST IS HEREBY EMPLOYED AND ENGAGED AND AGREES TO RENDER HIS SERVICES AS A MUSICIAN AND SINGER ON THE "LOUISIANA HAYRIDE" PROGRAM EVERY SATURDAY EVENING AT THE MUNICIPAL AUDITORIUM, SHREVEPORT, LOUISIANA, OR WHEREVER STATION MAY DESIGNATE, BETWEEN THE HOURS OF 8 P. M. AND 12 P. M.

4.

WHEN ARTIST IS REQUIRED TO RENDER HIS SERVICES AT A PER-
FORMANCE IN SOME CITY OTHER THAN SHREVEPORT, LOUISIANA, STATION SHALL
HAVE THE OPTION TO FURNISH TRANSPORTATION OF ITS OWN SELECTION TO
ARTIST OR TO FURNISH ARTIST TRANSPORTATION REIMBURSEMENT AT EIGHT CENTS
(8¢) PER ROAD MILE BETWEEN SHREVEPORT AND THE PLACE OF PERFORMANCE.
STATION SHALL NOT BE RESPONSIBLE FOR ANY OTHER EXPENSES WHEN OUT-OF-
TOWN PERFORMANCES ARE REQUIRED.

5.

ARTIST AGREES TO BE PROMPT AND APPEAR ON SAID PROGRAM EVERY
SATURDAY NIGHT, AND TO PERFORM HIS SERVICES TO THE BEST OF HIS ABILITY
IN A COMPETENT AND PAINS-TAKING MANNER, AND TO ABIDE BY ALL REASON-
ABLE RULES AND REGULATIONS OF STATION. STATION SHALL HAVE COMPLETE
CONTROL OVER THE PRESENTATION, DIRECTION, AND CONTENT OF ALL PROGRAMS,
INCLUDING THE NUMBER AND CHARACTER OF SELECTIONS TO BE RENDERED BY
ARTIST, BUT ARTIST SHALL FURNISH HIS OWN MUSICAL INSTRUMENTS AND
COSTUMES. ARTIST IS GIVEN THE RIGHT TO MISS one SATURDAY'S PERFORM-
ANCES DURING EACH 3 month PERIOD OF THIS CONTRACT UPON GIVING
FIFTEEN (15) DAYS' WRITTEN NOTICE TO STATION PRIOR TO THE PERFORMANCE
WHICH HE INTENDS TO MISS. THIS RIGHT SHALL NOT BE CUMULATIVE AND
ARTIST SHALL NOT BE ENTITLED TO ANY COMPENSATION FOR PERFORMANCE
NOT GIVEN.

6.

STATION SHALL HAVE THE RIGHT TO BROADCAST, TELEVISE, OR
RECORD SAID PROGRAM FOR IMMEDIATE OR FUTURE RELEASE AND BROADCAST
TO THE PUBLIC, AND SHALL HAVE THE RIGHT TO USE ARTIST'S NAME AND
PHOTOGRAPH FOR ADVERTISING, PROGRAM BILLING, OR PUBLICITY. STATION
SHALL NOT BE BOUND TO BROADCAST EVERY PERFORMANCE BUT SHALL BROADCAST
AT LEAST ONE-HALF OF ALL PERFORMANCES AND STATION SHALL HAVE THE RIGHT
TO BROADCAST SAID PERFORMANCES OVER ITS OWN FACILITIES OR AS MANY
STATIONS AS IT MAY ENGAGE.

7.

IN CONSIDERATION OF THE AFORESAID SERVICES AND EMPLOYMENT,
STATION SHALL PAY TO ARTIST NO LATER THAN MONDAY AFTER EACH PRECEDING
SATURDAY'S PERFORMANCE, THE SUM OF _____Union Scale_____
_____($) DOLLARS,
AND SAID SUM SHALL BE PAID ONLY IF THE ARTIST HAS ACTUALLY BEEN PRESENT

AND HAS PERFORMED AT THE PRECEDING SATURDAY'S PERFORMANCE. NO COM-
PENSATION SHALL BE PAID ARTIST IF HE MISSES THE PERFORMANCE FOR ANY
REASON, INCLUDING ILLNESS, OR UNAVOIDABLE OBSTACLE ON HIS PART.

8.

IN CONSIDERATION OF THE PUBLICITY WHICH WILL ACCRUE TO
ARTIST, AND IN CONSIDERATION OF THE AFORESAID FIRST YEAR'S EMPLOYMENT
AND THE REMUNERATION TO BE PAID, ALL OF WHICH ARTIST ACKNOWLEDGES TO
BE ADEQUATE CONSIDERATION FOR THE HEREINAFTER DESCRIBED OPTION,
STATION IS GIVEN THE OPTION TO RENEW AND EXTEND THIS CONTRACT FOR
A SECOND YEAR UPON THE SAME TERMS, CONDITIONS, AND SALARY, BEGIN-
NING IMMEDIATELY UPON TERMINATION OF THE FIRST YEAR, BY NOTIFYING
ARTIST OF ITS INTENTION TO RENEW AT LEAST FIFTEEN (15) DAYS PRIOR
TO THE END OF THE FIRST YEAR. ALSO, IN CONSIDERATION OF THE AFORE-
SAID AND IN CONSIDERATION OF THE SECOND YEAR'S EMPLOYMENT, STATION
IS GIVEN THE FURTHER OPTION TO RENEW THIS CONTRACT FOR A THIRD YEAR,
UPON THE SAME TERMS, CONDITIONS, AND SALARY, BEGINNING IMMEDIATELY,
UPON TERMINATION OF THE SECOND YEAR, BY NOTIFYING ARTIST OF ITS
INTENTION TO RENEW AT LEAST FIFTEEN (15) DAYS PRIOR TO THE END OF
THE SECOND YEAR.

9.

IF ARTIST IS PREVENTED BY ILLNESS, ACCIDENT OR ANY OTHER
CAUSE, FROM PERFORMING FOR ANY FOUR CONSECUTIVE PERFORMANCES, STATION
IS GIVEN THE RIGHT AT ITS SOLE OPTION, TO TERMINATE THIS CONTRACT
IMMEDIATELY.

10.

IN CONSIDERATION OF THE AFORESAID EMPLOYMENT, ARTIST HEREBY
AGREES AND COVENANTS THAT IF, AND IN THE EVENT, OF THE TERMINATION OF
EMPLOYMENT WITH STATION, HE WILL NOT, DIRECTLY OR INDIRECTLY, AS PRIN-
CIPAL, AGENT OR OTHERWISE, USE OR CAUSE TO BE USED IN ANY ADVERTISE-
MENT, THE WORDS, "KWKH" OR "LOUISIANA HAYRIDE" OR ANY IMITATION OR
APPROXIMATION OF THOSE WORDS. ARTIST FURTHER AGREES NOT TO ADVERTISE
HIMSELF, OR ANY GROUP WITH WHOM HE MAY WORK, AS HAVING "FORMERLY BEEN
WITH "KWKH" OR "LOUISIANA HAYRIDE", OR TO USE THE WORDS "KWKH" OR
"LOUISIANA HAYRIDE" IN ANY MANNER WHATSOEVER. ARTIST ACKNOWLEDGES
THAT THE WORDS "KWKH" AND "LOUISIANA HAYRIDE" ARE THE SOLE AND EX-
CLUSIVE PROPERTY OF STATION AND THAT IF HE SHOULD EVER VIOLATE THIS

AGREEMENT, HE SHALL BE LIABLE TO A SUIT FOR INJUNCTION AND DAMAGES.

11.

ARTIST ACKNOWLEDGES THAT HIS SERVICES ARE UNIQUE, AND HE
HEREBY AGREES AND COVENANTS NOT TO ACCEPT ANY EMPLOYMENT, AS
MUSICIAN OR SINGER, WHICH WILL INTERFERE WITH OR PROHIBIT HIS AP-
PEARANCE ON THE PROGRAM HEREIN SPECIFIED, AND THAT IN THE EVENT OF
HIS FAILURE TO COMPLY WITH THIS CONTRACT, AND IN ADDITION TO THE
LIABILITY FOR ALL DAMAGES CAUSED TO STATION, ARTIST CAN BE RESTRAINED
BY INJUNCTION FROM PROCEEDING WITH SAID OTHER EMPLOYMENT DURING
THE PERIOD OF THIS CONTRACT UP TO AND INCLUDING_____

_____6 November 1955_____

IN WITNESS WHEREOF THIS AGREEMENT IS EXECUTED IN DUPLICATE
ORIGINALS THIS 6th DAY OF_____November_____, 19 54 .

WITNESSES: STATION
                                              INTERNATIONAL BROADCASTING CORP.

Vernon E Presley   BY *H. L. Fryar*
Gladys Presley   ARTIST

                                              † *Elvis Presley*

                                              † *Winfield Scott Moore*

                                              † *William Black*

One place he didn't go with it, though, was the Lake Cliff Club just outside of Shreveport. The honky tonk had been the regular Friday night spot of popular Hayriders Hoot & Curley when, on November 19th, Elvis and the boys were asked to fill in on short notice. Needless to say, the hard and fast country audience wanted no part of "That's All Right, Mama," and by the end of the first set, the joint was all but deserted. The Lake Cliff Club, however, would soon prove to be the exception rather than the rule.

LAKE CLIFF CLUB AD
FOR ELVIS "PRESSLEY"
NOVEMBER 19, 1954

Throughout December, Elvis, Scotty and Bill traveled back and forth from Memphis, playing gigs in nearby Helena, Arkansas; Corinth, Mississippi; and Gladewater, Texas. Billboard Magazine called the act "the hottest piece of merchandise on the Louisiana Hayride" and cited Elvis as "the youngster with the hillbilly blues beat." "Shake, Rattle and Roll" and "Hearts Of Stone", two current rhythm and blues hits, were added to their song list and "Milkcow Boogie Blues" became Elvis' third release on Sun Records.

Tom Perryman, disc jockey and promoter at KSIJ in nearby Gladewater, Texas soon added Elvis and band to his tour package of Hayride stars Jim Ed & Maxine Brown, Caroline Bradshaw, the Rowley Trio and others. They worked mostly in the East Texas area.

"Something that people don't know," he told me, "it is the way we worked with Elvis, Scotty & Bill, Jim Ed and Maxine." What we would do is we would book the date, I'd pay the sponsor maybe 15 or 20% - like a school or something - for the auditorium. Then we'd pay the musicians and then pay the advertising - most all the advertising was me on the radio station with a few newspaper ads and placards. We took all that off of the top. Then I would take 15% of what was left. Elvis would take half the remainder and he would split it with Scotty and Bill, and

JOYCE RAILSBACK'S DIARY FOR
DECEMBER 18, 1954

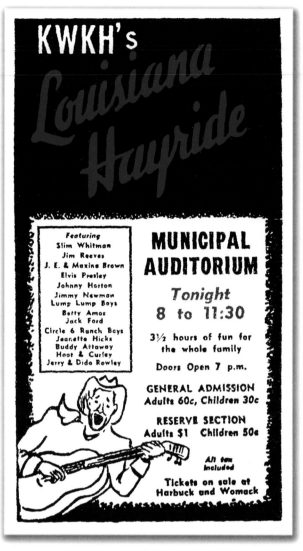

LOUISIANA HAYRIDE SHOW
NOVEMBER 6, 1954

own houses and everything in those camps and had a little community center. On the front row was a grandmother, her daughter and granddaughter - three generations on the front row of Elvis' show, and I got to watching them. And every one of them had the same reaction. Y'know, just spontaneous, and I thought to myself, then I said, 'I don't know what it is but this kid has got something.' That's how I describe the effect that Elvis had even in his very early days. And you saw what happened... He worked with all of those guys like the same he worked with me in that era. That's the way we worked in those days."

"One tour I remember. It was the first week of January, 1955. I booked Elvis to go with Billy Walker, Jimmy & Johnny and me. We did shows in San Angelo, Lubbock and Midland. Joe Treadway at KPEP ran an ad for the San Angelo show headlined by "Alvis" Presley. I was doing comedy under the name "Peach Seed Jones," and he had me listed with "If You Don't Someone Else Will," which was Jimmy & Johnny's hit. He didn't even mention them. That was pretty funny to us," Tillman Franks told me.

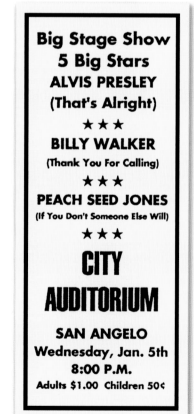

I'd give the other half to Jim Ed & Maxine. I promoted them something like 17 dates in less than one year. They'd come to Gladewater and spend a week at a time. We'd work school houses, rodeo arenas, ball parks, anywhere."

"...And I always watched the audience to see what the response would be, from every act I booked so I could see if I wanted to book them again. We played a little community center in the town of Hawkins, Texas which was the Humble Oil camp. In those days they had their

(RIGHT) THE "BIG STAGE SHOW" AT THE CITY AUDITORIUM IN SAN ANGELO FEATURED "ALVIS" PRESLEY, BILLY WALKER, AND HAYRIDE BASS PLAYER TILLMAN FRANKS AS COMIC "PEACH SEED JONES" - **JANUARY 5, 1955.**

Tonight!
Elvis Presley

Mint Club
GLADEWATER

NOV 54

(CLOCKWISE FROM TOP LEFT) AT THE MINT CLUB IN GLADEWATER, TEXAS, ELVIS POSES WITH HAYRIDE FAN ANN PAULSEN; ELVIS, SCOTTY & BILL ON STAGE; ELVIS GETS A HUG FROM FELLOW HAYRIDER TIBBY EDWARDS - **NOVEMBER 22, 1954.**

TOM PERRYMAN

Tom Perryman
DJ & Hayride promoter
1952-60

"Every time Elvis and them would come to my house, Billie, my wife, would make a great big ol' crock - an old country milk crock, full of banana pudding and he'd eat it until he couldn't hardly walk."

JAN 55

ELVIS ON STAGE AT THE MAYFAIR BUILDING, TYLER, TEXAS FAIRGROUNDS - **JANUARY 25, 1955.**

JOYCE RAILSBACK'S DIARY FOR
ELVIS' 20TH BIRTHDAY - **JANUARY 8, 1955**

"When we got to Lubbock, we played Fair Park. Waylon Jennings was a DJ back then and he came to the show. The next night we tore 'em up in Midland. There was more than 1600 people in the audience. You could see they liked what Elvis was doing."

The following night, Elvis spent his twentieth birthday with us on the Hayride. He was sporting pink crocodile skin shoes. The Memphis Flash turned in a rousing performance that left Joyce Railsback writing and underlining, "This guy I'd like to meet!"

Elvis was quite the colorful character. The following week he took the stage wearing a rust colored suit, a purple tie with black dots, and pink socks. He took the stage that night shortly after 8:30. Jim Reeves had just tried out "The Wilder Your

Heart Beats, The Sweeter Your Love" and Elvis chose to open with "Hearts of Stone", the popular R&B number he'd learned a few weeks earlier. He followed it with his standard, "That's All Right, Mama" and encored with "Tweedlee Dee," another rhythm and blues song that had charted that very morning for Lavern Baker. Hayride staff musicians Jimmy Day on steel and Floyd Cramer on piano were added to the mix. Floyd's trademark slip note playing and honky tonk stylings appealed to Elvis and the two would record often in the future.

Hayride favorite Johnny Horton came out next and, in what was perhaps the first formal tribute to the young entertainer, covered "Fool, Fool, Fool," and credited it as Elvis Presley's song.

Sitting in the audience that fateful evening and taking it all in for the first time was a man who would soon be linked to Elvis forever; a former carnival barker and current manager of Eddy Arnold that went by the title of "Colonel"... Tom Parker. The Colonel, undoubtedly, couldn't help but be impressed.

"COLONEL" TOM PARKER

BILLY WALKER

*Billy Walker
Hayride cast member
1952-56*

"I took [Elvis] on a tour with me in the first week of January, 1955 out to West Texas, and in Midland - on January 7th we played Midland and I gave him a lil ol' Hostess cupcake with a candle in the middle of it and we sang Happy Birthday to him for his 20th birthday."

ELVIS ON THE HAYRIDE STAGE FOR HIS 20TH BIRTHDAY - **JANUARY 8, 1955.**

Elvis returned the following weekend, January 22, and turned in another crowd-pleasing performance. Once again, the addition of steel guitar and piano, this time by Hayride musicians Sonny Trammel and Leon Post, brought a slightly different interpretation to the now routine "That's All Right, Mama" and "Blue Moon Of Kentucky." Elvis added "Money, Honey," another popular rhythm and blues number that had been a hit for the Drifters and took a run at "I Don't Care If The Sun Don't Shine," the flip side of his second Sun Record, "Good Rockin' Tonight." Surprisingly enough, "I Don't Care" had actually been written for the Walt Disney animated classic "Cinderella," but had failed to make the final cut. It was reworked in the early fifties by Patti Page and popular crooner Dean Martin. Being a big fan of Dino's, Elvis drew inspiration from Martin's lazy delivery of the song.

For the next several weeks, Elvis and band played a number of dates in Texas, Arkansas, Mississippi and Louisiana. This was the primary area of influence for Sam Phillips' distribution network and became the stronghold of Presley fans. The circuit included a stop off in Lubbock, Texas on February the 13th, where Elvis was billed as the "be-bop western star of the Louisiana Hayride," and shared the stage with Hank Snow's son, Jimmie Rodgers Snow. The opening act was a popular local country-western duo, Buddy and Bob... Buddy Holly, that is.

By now, the career choice of musician was starting to pay off for the hard-working trio. Though they played the Hayride just two Saturdays in February and three in March, the band's income went from $2,000 in January to a high of $5,000 in March before settling in around $1,000 a week. Colonel Parker helped book them on Hank Snow's tour beginning in mid-February, and with each performance, Elvis' confidence and popularity grew by leaps and bounds.

Living in Shreveport most weekends, Elvis stayed primarily in motels. They were called "tourist courts" in those days and the Al-Ida Motel and the Shirley Temple Courts were his frequent haunts. George Dement, Bossier City's mayor, was a cook back then at the grill alongside the Al-Ida and remembers Elvis as a polite young man who never passed up an opportunity to preen himself in the mirror of the cigarette machine. George loaned Elvis a pillow one time for the long ride back to Memphis and will tell you to this day he never got his pillow back!

JOYCE RAILSBACK'S DIARY FOR
JANUARY 15, 1955

ELVIS ON THE HAYRIDE STAGE - **JANUARY 22, 1955**

ELVIS ON THE HAYRIDE STAGE - **JANUARY 22, 1955**

ELVIS AND HAYRIDE STEEL PLAYER JIMMY DAY ON STAGE AT THE MAYFAIR BUILDING, TYLER, TEXAS - **JANUARY 25, 1955**

ELVIS HAS A COKE AND A SMOKE BACKSTAGE AT THE MAYFAIR.

Vera "Dido" Rowley
Hayride cast member
1952-55

DIDO ROWLEY

"I remember one Saturday night at the Hayride. Jim Reeves had gone to California for a screen test and I was sitting backstage with Elvis. He asked me, 'You ever think I'll get a screen test?' I told him, 'Sure.   You'll be the biggest star ever.' He was flabbergasted. 'You really think so?' I said 'It's written all over you'."

THE AL-IDA MOTEL ACROSS THE RIVER
IN BOSSIER CITY.

On Saturdays Elvis would often have breakfast with Stan Lewis, owner of a prominent local record shop and a key player in the region's music scene: "I was a distributor for most every independent label, retail store, one stops, and jukebox operators there were at that particular time. When Sam Phillips sent me the record "That's All Right, Mama" when it was released by Elvis Presley, it was the changing of rockabilly music. It was something different; a new sound."

Stan told me he got stuck with the check a time or two for the often broke teenager, but Elvis would return the favor by holding autograph parties at Stan's Record Shop on Texas Street.

Early on, Elvis kept company with Carolyn Bradshaw, a petite big-eyed brunette who also performed on the Hayride. He most often could be found playing the pinball machine at Murrell Stansell's Bantam Grill or mixing it up at Harry's Barbecue, a favorite hangout of George Jones, Faron Young, Johnny Cash and others. If a good movie hit town, Elvis headed down to the Strand or Don Theaters.

By mid-March, Elvis was spending more weekends away from the Hayride than he was on. The Colonel continued to line up   venues for him to play and the Hayride booked him out in some of their package shows in the area. Elvis had become quite comfortable on stage by this time and would often tell off-color jokes or make flippant remarks as he sought to find a level of comfort with his increasing audience of teenage fans. The hip and leg gyrations were a natural by-product of his seemingly endless supply of energy. He was possessed and driven by a spirit few understood but all were quick to recognize as a force to be reckoned with.

JOYCE RAILSBACK'S DIARY FOR
FEBRUARY 5, 1955

My fellow Hayride announcer, Norm Bale, remembers the audience reactions to Elvis: "He knew he was different and right away, the girls especially would come running down to the stage. We'd always let them come down and take pictures and ask for autographs and this kind of thing as long as they didn't disrupt the show. But when Elvis came on, right from the start they'd come flooding down to the stage when he was there, hootin' and hollerin'."

On March 19th, 1955, Elvis found himself double booked. The Hayride was doing a road show at College Station but Elvis was also scheduled to appear at the Eagles Hall club in Houston as part of a three concert promotion by Houston disc jockey Biff Collie. Listed fourth on the Hayride bill behind Flatt & Scruggs, Little Jimmie Dickens and Archie Campbell, Elvis and the boys did their songs quickly, then drove like mad for Houston. They took the stage that night at Eagles Hall and after some good-natured clowning, Elvis unleashed a wild and chaotic performance that even on tape was palpable. It is not hard to imagine his shoulders hunching forward and his

HAYRIDE STAR CAROLYN BRADSHAW

JOYCE RAILSBACK'S DIARY FOR
MARCH 5, 1955

STAN LEWIS

*Stan Lewis
Hayride record distributor
1948-60*

"Elvis was a real fine, young, well-mannered kid and he loved gospel records...and he loved the blues. He would come up to my shop and listen to the records. I'd sometimes take him out to Sansone's on Spring Street on Saturday morning and buy his breakfast, 'cause he was broke at the time, and then he'd go his way with Bill and Scotty and DJ.

After Ed Sullivan, he came back for autograph parties and it was just a mob scene. It was just unbelievable. The traffic, and the police outside. They just almost tore up my record shop, not literally tore it up, there was just so many people in there and pulling records out and listening to 'em... The kid was just great in those days... just a super kid."

MAY 55

ELVIS AND HIS HAYRIDE SWEETIE, CAROLYN BRADSHAW, BACKSTAGE AT THE HAYRIDE.
MAY 21, 1955

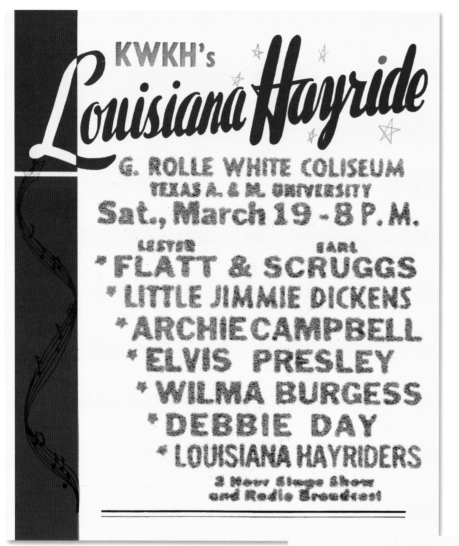

Throughout the month of April, Elvis criss-crossed the state of Texas, playing high schools in towns like Breckenridge, Stamford and Seymour; and venues ranging in size from the Hayride-sized Sportatorium in Dallas, home to the Big D Jamboree, down to an intimate setting at Owl Park in Gainesville. Back in Shreveport, the month long "Holiday In Dixie" social cotillion and festival was in full swing, occupying the Municipal Auditorium as it did each year and forcing the Hayride out on the road for most of the month. Remote shows were broadcast from Houston on the 2nd, Waco on the 23rd, and Gladewater on the 30th.

POSTER FOR THE COLLEGE STATION HAYRIDE SHOW - **MARCH 19, 1955.**

head slamming back as he shouted at Scotty and Bill, "Let's rock!" and began his trance-like delivery of "Good Rockin' Tonight." Breathless and moving to a rhythm all of his own, Elvis followed up with Ray Charles' current hit "I Got a Woman," which sent many teenage girls into orbit. Yet, the following week Elvis journeyed to New York and was turned down cold by Arthur Godfrey's Talent Scouts, a popular rival of the Ed Sullivan Show. How they could fail to find a pulse on this young man is beyond me.

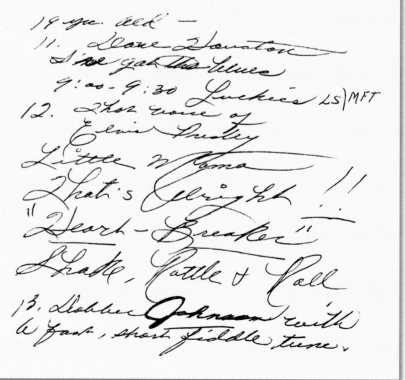

JOYCE RAILSBACK'S DIARY FOR **APRIL 2, 1955**

As young men were given to do, Elvis had a propensity for speeding and was nabbed just outside of Shreveport on the way back from the Houston gig. Snug behind the wheel of his flashy new pink Cadillac, he was pursued by a state trooper for nearly nine miles up Mansfield Road at speeds described by the curiously named Officer Strange as "exceeding 80 miles per hour." "Subject" was then carried to the Caddo Parish Jail where he bonded out at $25.00.

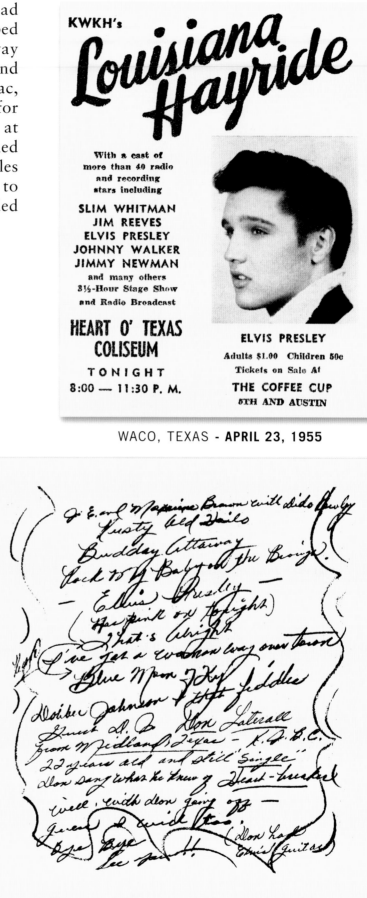

WACO, TEXAS - **APRIL 23, 1955**

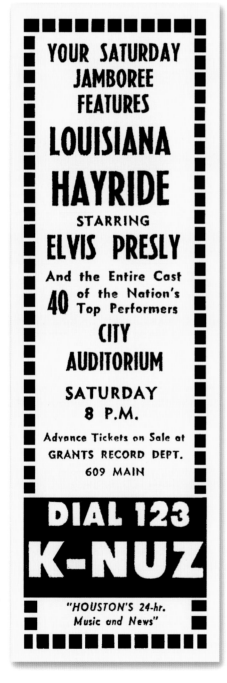

HOUSTON - **APRIL 2, 1955**

JOYCE RAILSBACK'S DIARY FOR
APRIL 9, 1955

AT THE HAYRIDE IN SHREVEPORT (CLOCKWISE FROM TOP RIGHT), ELVIS POSES WITH JIMMY RODGERS SNOW; LAYS IT OUT ON THE GUITAR; AND POSES WITH TWO YOUNG FANS. (AT LEFT) A TYPICAL POSTER OF THE ERA - **APRIL 9, 1955.**

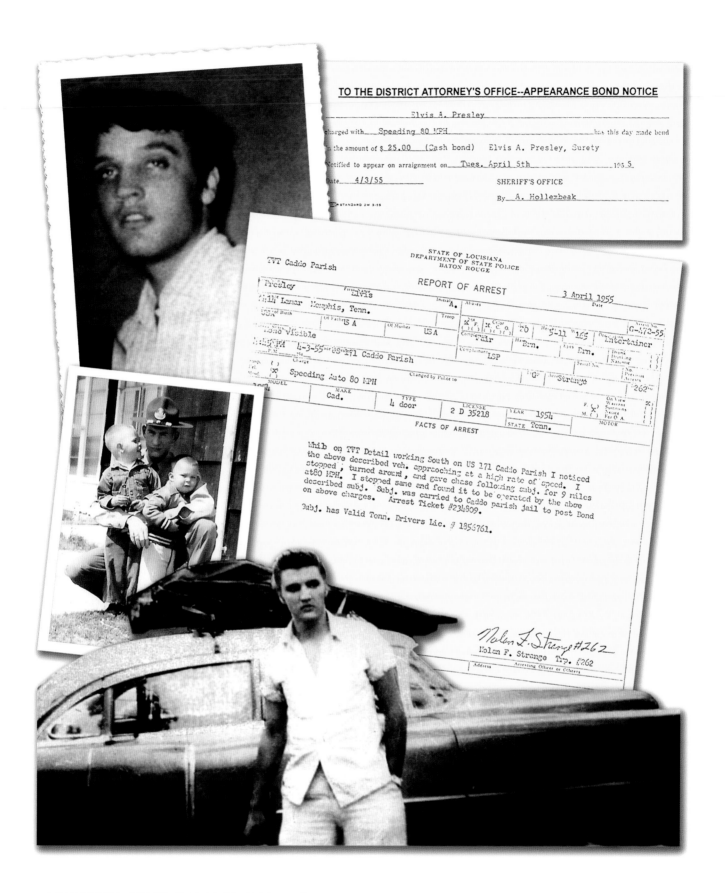

STATE OF LOUISIANA
DEPARTMENT OF STATE POLICE
BATON ROUGE

TVT Caddo Parish

REPORT OF ARREST 3 April 1955
Date

Presley Elvis Initial A. Alias Arrest No. G-472-55

Phillip Lamar Memphis, Tenn.

USA Of Father US A Of Mother USA Troop Sex M. Color W C.O. 20 Height 5-11 Weight 165 Occupation Entertainer

None Visible Complexion Fair Hair Brn. Eyes Brn.

4-3-55 85 171 Caddo Parish Complainant LSP

Charge Changed by Police to Arrested by Strange 262

Speeding Auto 80 MPH

MAKE Cad. TYPE 4 door LICENSE 2 D 35218 YEAR 1954 STATE Tenn.

FACTS OF ARREST

While on TVT Detail working South on US 171 Caddo Parish I noticed the above described veh. approaching at a high rate of speed. I stopped, turned around, and gave chase following subj. for 9 miles at 80 MPH. I stopped same and found it to be operated by the above described subj. Subj. was carried to Caddo parish jail to post Bond on above charges. Arrest Ticket #234809.

Subj. has Valid Tenn. Drivers Lic. # 1856761.

Nolan F. Strange #262
Nolan F. Strange Trp. #262
Address Arresting Officer or Officers

LOUISIANA STATE TROOPER NOLAN STRANGE, A FAMILY MAN, DIDN'T KNOW WHO ELVIS WAS WHEN HE STOPPED THE KING FOR SPEEDING ON SHREVEPORT'S MANSFIELD ROAD. "HE WAS AS NICE AS COULD BE EXPECTED, CUTTIN' UP WITH THE BOYS IN THE BACK WHO WERE GIVING HIM GRIEF" - **APRIL OF 1955.**

ELVIS PRESLEY

Elvis Presley is one of the Louisiana Hayride artists that will take part in the two-day Jimmy Rodgers Memorial Celebration at Meridian May 25 and 26. This young recording artist has been received with tremendous enthusiasm on his many personal appearances the past several months and is well on his way toward becoming one of the top artists in the nation. Appearing with him will be Scotty and Bill, the two musicians whose unique musical arrangements have contributed so much to Elvis' style of singing.

MERIDIAN, MISSISSIPPI
MAY, 1955

Christmas came early that year for Joyce Railsback. The West Texas teen got to meet the man of her dreams on April 26th when Elvis played the City Auditorium in her home town of Big Spring. She remembers him wearing pink pants and a pink shirt with black trim. After the show, Joyce approached Elvis and, awed into silence, handed him a Hayride program to autograph. Over the newspaper photo she had glued to the back cover he wrote, "Yours, Elvis Presley," and handed it back to her.

Joyce managed a "thank you" to which Elvis firmly replied "Well, thank you!" With those words, another spell was cast and another teenage girl was left floating on air.

Four days later, Elvis' dream machine began giving him fits and broke down en route to the Gladewater Hayride show. He got it running again but barely made the final curtain call. An instrumental usually closed out each show and Floyd Cramer had just premiered his new piano song "Fancy Pants" when Horace Logan made the call to squeeze the ever-popular Memphis Flash into the waning moments of the broadcast. Clearly dejected, Elvis managed a half-hearted rendition of "Tweedlee Dee."

The trio played the Louisiana Hayride only once in May of 1955, but made three of four Saturdays in June amid a flurry of mostly Texas and Mississippi dates. Early June saw the demise of young Presley's precious pink Cadillac when it caught fire in Fulton, Arkansas while the group was en route to Texarkana. On the 25th, Elvis was back at the Hayride and came on stage shortly after a crew cut bug-eyed disc jockey from Houston. George Jones was the fella's name and one could easily see why they'd taken to calling him "Possum." The 23-year old was making his Louisiana Hayride debut that evening and would return in the fall for a seven month stint, kicking off his own climb to stardom.

"THE POSSUM"
GEORGE JONES

AN AD FOR THE HAYRIDE'S ARTIST SERVICE BUREAU FROM THE SPRING OF 1955 LISTED ELVIS AMONG THE SHOW'S STARS.

AT THE HAYRIDE (CLOCKWISE FROM TOP RIGHT) ELVIS POSES BACKSTAGE WITH HIS COUSIN, GENE SMITH; ELVIS SPORTS A ONE-TIME "PERM" LOOK WHICH DOESN'T LAST; ON STAGE; GRACEFULLY EMERGING FROM THE BATHROOM - **MAY 21, 1955.**

Elvis began his portion of the show with another R&B favorite, "Baby, Let's Play House," a song religious leaders of the era blasted as encouraging "premarital relations." His performance was spirited but tinged with a bit of cruel irony as he sang the lyric he'd changed months earlier from "You may have religion" to "You may have a pink Cadillac." Next on the menu was "Good Rockin' Tonight" and the ever-popular "Blue Moon of Kentucky." Scotty and Bill followed with an instrumental, working out "Meet Mr. Calahan" with Floyd Cramer and Jimmy Day. David Houston, Johnny Horton, Tibby Edwards and the Browns rounded out an all-star Hayride cast for the evening.

July 16, 1955 was a special day for Elvis. He was bolstered with the news that "Baby, Let's Play House," his fourth Sun single, had entered Cash Box's Country & Western chart that afternoon at Number 15, marking his first appearance on the national charts. Elvis was with us that evening and, in celebration, he shared with the Hayride audience the flip side of that first chart record, "You're Right, I'm Left, She's Gone."

As August got underway in 1955, Colonel Tom Parker continued to worm his way into the affairs of Elvis and his manager, Bob Neal. The Colonel had been instrumental in securing many bookings for the group, most notably the Hank Snow tour, and pressured Elvis and his parents into signing an agreement that established Parker as a "special advisor" to Elvis and Bob Neal. He was, in theory, to help in any way to build up the career of Elvis and promote him throughout the southwest. The Colonel retained the exclusive promotional rights to many

JOYCE RAILSBACK'S DIARY FOR
FEBRUARY 5, 1955

cities and began to steer the Presley career as he saw fit.

Meanwhile, Elvis began stealing the show in bookings with former Hayride Star Webb Pierce and current Hayrider Sonny James. Elvis and his fellow Sun recording artist, newcomer Johnny Cash, garnered far more of the spotlight than their secondary billing anticipated during appearances in Sheffield, Alabama and Camden, Arkansas. On August fifth he triumphantly returned to the Overton Park Shell in Memphis where one year earlier he'd launched his career from obscurity alongside Hayride regulars Slim Whitman and Billy Walker. This time Elvis was a prominent headliner and the crowd of 4,000 jammed the shell and erupted in waves of screams. Webb was heard to comment later: "Unless we learn to keep up with him, that kid may put us all out of a job before it's over."

(ABOVE) AT THE HAYRIDE: ELVIS BELTS OUT HIS FIRST NATIONAL CHART HITS, "YOU'RE RIGHT, I'M LEFT, SHE'S GONE" AND "BABY, LET'S PLAY HOUSE" FOR THE EXCITED FANS. (LOWER LEFT) ELVIS' MANAGER, BOB NEAL, A FORMER SHREVEPORT DISC JOCKEY, WORKED HARD TO PROMOTE HIS RISING STAR BUT WAS SOON CROWDED OUT BY THE OVERBEARING COLONEL PARKER - JULY 16, 1955.

It was readily apparent that Elvis' world had changed dramatically. The confidence that had fluctuated with each move up and down the local charts was steadied by his newfound national success. By the end of his first year with the Louisiana Hayride, Elvis was hotter than a two dollar pistol. During this period, Hayride staff drummer D. J. Fontana was added to the Presley ensemble. On September the eighth, Elvis signed on for another year with the Hayride, this time receiving $200 per week and being allowed to miss one Saturday every two months. Despite the vocal objections of Colonel Parker, who felt a major record deal was just around the corner, the cautious Vernon and Gladys Presley once again opted to co-sign the Hayride contract for their 20-year old son. On November the 11th, the renewal took hold and the following day, Elvis was named "Most Promising Country & Western Artist" in the annual Disc Jockey Poll. Barely a week later, Colonel Parker finalized the sale of Elvis' Sun Records contract to RCA for the healthy sum of $35,000.

Jimmy Lee Fautheree, half of the Hayride duo Jimmy & Johnny, told me a story about that: "I thought it was real funny when he first - after he caught on real good, he was telling me and my wife about Colonel Parker selling his contract to Victor, and said... as rich as he got, y'know, buying Cadillacs for people, but this time he said, 'And they gave me $5000!' So, that was kinda funny to me, later on, with him being so wealthy."

As 1955 drew to a close, Elvis was poised on the verge of national stardom. The Colonel booked him for a series of appearances in the new year on CBS television's Saturday night variety program, "Stage Show," hosted by Jimmy and Tommy Dorsey, and RCA re-released five of the earlier Sun recordings.

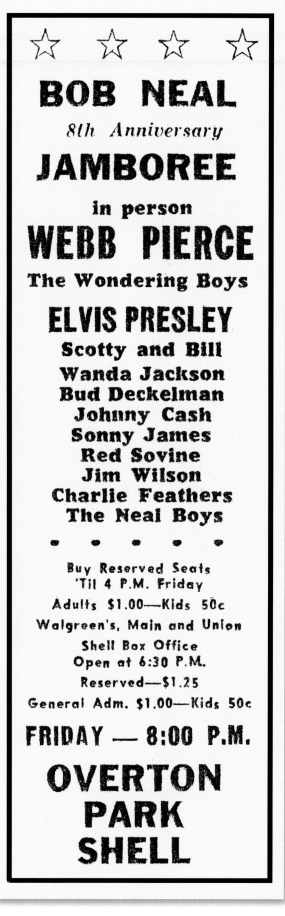

THE MEMPHIS TRIUMPH - **AUGUST 5, 1955**

JUN 55

ELVIS AND CAROLYN BRADSHAW BACKSTAGE AT THE HAYRIDE - **JUNE 25, 1955**

AT THE LOUISIANA HAYRIDE - **JULY 2, 1955**

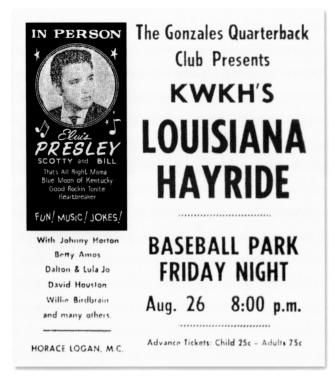

GONZALES, TEXAS - **AUGUST 26, 1955**

In retrospect, one of the most star-studded Louisiana Hayride shows ever occurred on December 31st. Elvis topped the bill for the New Year's Eve program that included Johnny Horton, David Houston, George Jones and special guests Johnny Cash and the Tennessee Two. Cash and Jones had signed onto the Hayride the previous month and would share the stage with Elvis for the first quarter of 1956. Folks in attendance that memorable evening definitely got their sixty cents worth!

RENEWS CONTRACT— Elvis Presley, Louisiana Hayride artist and Sun recording star, last week renewed his Hayride contract for one year. Elvis, who won a wide following with his unusual singing style, now has three records occupying four positions on the nation's country music popularity charts.

HAYRIDE STAR DAVID HOUSTON WITH FUTURE ELVIS GUITARIST JAMES BURTON

SHREVEPORT TIMES - **SEPTEMBER 18, 1955**

JIMMY LEE

Jimmy Lee Fautheree
Hayride cast member
1951-60

"We would do some of that rock and roll, but we didn't want to feature it, and Horace Logan used to laugh about it. He said Elvis wouldn't follow us on the stage 'cause we'd do that rock and roll stuff first before he got out there to do it. So, we had to quit it and let him come on first."

Johnny Cash used to stand in the wings and watch Elvis perform and Elvis would stand in the wings and watch Johnny perform. Who picked up what from whom, I don't know. But artists were prone to do that. They would go out and stand in the audience or stand in one of the doorways and look out and see how the other person was being accepted. I'm sure they learned things from each other that they couldn't do on the Hayride but they might do at a show they were going on the road.

Jeanette Hicks recalled there were times that Elvis would poke his head out from behind the curtain and look out and the audience was just looking for him, especially these girls down front, and they'd see him and they'd scream, "Well, you can just imagine that whoever it was - Johnny Cash, whoever it was on stage, they didn't care for that and so Horace had to put a stop to that."

THE MAN IN BLACK, HAYRIDE STAR JOHNNY CASH

Elvis made the first of four consecutive weekly television appearances on "Stage Show" at the end of January. In this earliest of live footage, it became clear to anyone watching that Elvis Presley was a true pop phenomenon. For the first time, the nation was introduced visually to his unique style of rhythm and blues delivered with a touch of bravado.

JOYCE RAILSBACK'S DIARY FOR - **DECEMBER 17, 1955**

KWKH'S
Louisiana Hayride

Tonight
8:00 till 11:30 P.M.
MUNICIPAL AUDITORIUM

featuring:
ELVIS PRESLEY
JACK FORD • HOOT and CURLEY
BUZZ BUZBY and the Bayou Boys
JEANETTE HICKS
WERLY FAIRBURN
JOHNNY HORTON • GEORGE JONES
BUDDY ATTAWAY • DAVID HOUSTON
BETTY AMOS

With Special Guests
JOHNNY CASH and the
TENNESSEE TWO
and Many Others!

General Admission
Adults 60c   Children 30c
Reserve Section
Adults $1.00   Children 50c
Tax Included

Tickets
on Sale at
HARBUCK
& WOMACK

DEC 55

JOHNNY CASH AND ELVIS PRESLEY WERE BUT TWO OF THE SENSATIONAL ACTS ON HAND FOR THE HAYRIDE'S STAR STUDDED NEW YEAR'S EVE SHOW IN SHREVEPORT - **DECEMBER 31, 1955.**

JEANETTE HICKS

Jeanette Hicks
Hayride Cast Member
1953-57

"Elvis was one good looking man. Those eyes! He liked to play peek-a-boo. He used to sneak up behind me backstage, cover my eyes and say 'Guess who?' in a funny voice. Well, there was no mistaking who it was!"

KWKH'S
Louisiana Hayride

Tonight
8:00 till 11:30 P.M.
MUNICIPAL AUDITORIUM

featuring
Elvis Presley
Jimmie Newman ★ Wirly Fairburn
J. E. and Maxine Brown
David Houston ★ Buddy Attaway
Jeanette Hicks
Billy Walker ★ Floyd Cramer
Jimmy and Lenny Lee
Betty Amos ★ Jimmie Day

AND MANY OTHERS

General Admission
Adults 60c   Children 30c
Reserve Section
Adults $1.00   Children .50c

Tickets
on Sale at
HARBUCK
& WOMACK

Tax Included

By the third show, however, as the trumpets and trombones of the Dorsey Brothers orchestra crashed on top of his newest song, "Heartbreak Hotel," the Memphis Flash seemed irritated and lost; unable to find the beat he created in his mind and sang from his heart. Looking back, the show is both prophetic and sad in its foreshadowing of the movie and Vegas careers to come and the taming of this once free spirit.

The Saturday following his fourth "Stage Show" performance, Elvis returned to the Hayride and performed "Heartbreak Hotel" for the local audience who were, at once, thrilled. There were no trumpets blaring, no trombones... just Elvis and Scotty and Bill and DJ. As the crowd erupted like it never had before, a sense that the big time had arrived swept the Auditorium and touched each and every one of us, especially Hayride artist Betty Amos. Elvis would often borrow her guitar when his broke a string, and that night it happened again.

HAYRIDE—CRADLE OF STARS

THE LOUISIANA HAYRIDE, broadcast every Saturday night over KWKH from the Municipal Auditorium, has produced another recording star. RCA Victor recently purchased ELVIS PRESLEY'S contract from Sun Records for $40,000. His first release under the new label is already on sale. He will record Western, country, popular and rhythm in blues releases under his new contract.

SPOTLIGHT MAGAZINE
JANUARY, 1956

HAYRIDE STAR JIM REEVES

"He thrashed my guitar to death!" she relates. "I had a guitar, and I have a picture of it, and there's this place on the front of it. You can tell it's been beat to death, and I said 'I didn't do that. Elvis did that.' He took my guitar out there and absolutely thrashed it to death."

Like Hank Williams before him and Webb Pierce and Slim Whitman and Jim Reeves, Elvis was about to be ripped from the "Cradle of the Stars" and thrust into the international spotlight. We could look ahead to George Jones or Johnny Cash as the next Hayride star but already we knew no one would ever be the next Elvis Presley.

Hayride Star Week's Top Disc Artist

ELVIS PRESLEY . . . The KWKH Louisiana Hayride star is making Perry Como look to his laurels on RCA-Victor disc hits.

According to the March 3 issue of Billboard magazine, Louisiana Hayride star Elvis Presley is "the hottest artist on the RCA-Victor label this week."

The magazine goes on to point out that of the company's list of 25 best sellers six are by Presley and that his recording of "Heartbreak Hotel" and "I Was the One," is No. 2 on the list, right behind Perry Como's "Juke Box Baby."

"Heartbreak Hotel," although it was released only a couple of weeks ago, is already on the Billboard popularity charts, and Presley's recording of "I Forgot to Remember to Forget" holds the No. 1 spot as the nation's top country music record.

Presley's rise has been phenomenal since he joined the Hayride, about 18 months ago. Recently he was featured guest on Jackie Gleason's coast-to-coast television program, "The Stage Show," with Tommy and Jimmy Dorsey, for four consecutive weeks. According to the network stations, he drew an unprecedented amount of mail and as a result, he has been signed for two more appearances on the show, March 17 and 24.

Thus, another name has been added to the long list of artists for whom the Louisiana Hayride has been a springboard to fame. This list includes such favorites as the late Hank Williams, Webb Pierce, Faron Young, Slim Whitman, Jim Reeves and many others, but Elvis Presley promises to outstrip them all.

demand of "the final say" in the decision making process. Management of the Hayride would not, could not, afford to surrender control of the program at any price.

Ultimately, we knew we could hold this rising star no longer. So, in early April of 1956, Elvis was allowed to buy out the remaining six months of his contract for the sum of $10,000. He had performed three Hayride dates in March and his appearance on the 31st was allowed to be his last. Under the terms of his buyout agreement, however, it was stipulated Elvis would do one more Hayride show at a later date with the proceeds to benefit the charity of his choice.

As the television and movie offers began to pour in, it became increasingly difficult for Elvis and company to return to Shreveport each Saturday night. Colonel Parker, by now in complete control of Presley's career, tried everything in his power to relieve Elvis of his Hayride obligation. At one point, the Colonel offered to buy into the show and might just have pulled it off had it not come down to his

JOYCE RAILSBACK'S DIARY FOR ELVIS' LAST REGULAR HAYRIDE SHOW - **MARCH 31, 1956.**

BETTY AMOS

Betty Amos
Hayride cast member
1952-57

"I was very fond of Elvis but sometimes I didn't like him very much. He could be sweet, gentle, kind and thoughtful, but perplexing and aggravating too. He was sexy, handsome, childish and at times, downright cruel. He'd hit me and I'd hit him. Looking back, I suppose in all probability I was the closest he ever came to having a sister."

"Elvis was forever busting guitar strings. He'd run up to me and say 'Betty, quick, can I borrow your guitar?' He'd grab it and run out on stage..."

APR   55

RADIO STATION

KWKH

W. H. BRONSON, President
HENRY B. CLAY, Exec. Vice Pres. and Gen. Mgr.

50,000 WATTS ★ CBS RADIO

SHREVEPORT, LOUISIANA

To all to whom these Presents shall come or may Concern,

Greeting: *KNOW YE, That* INTERNATIONAL BROADCASTING CORPORATION, A Louisiana Corporation, licensor and operator of Radio Station KWKH, represented by H.L. Logan

XXXXXXXXXXX XXXXXXXXXXXXXXXXXXXXXXXXXXXXX XX XXXX XX XXXXXXXXX

for and in consideration of the sum of Ten Thousand . . . . *dollars ($* 10,000) *lawful money of the United States of America*

to it in hand paid by ELVIS PRESLEY

the receipt whereof is hereby acknowledged, has remised, released and forever discharged, and by these presents does for itself and its successors, remise, release and forever discharge the said

ELVIS PRESLEY, his

heirs, executors and administrators XXXXXXXXXX *and assigns of and from all, and all manner of action and actions, cause and causes of action, suits, debts, dues, sums of money, accounts, reckoning, bonds, bills, specialties, covenants, contracts, controversies, agreements, promises, variances, trespasses, damages, judgments, extents, executions, claims and demands whatsoever, in law, in admiralty, or in equity, which against* them,

it ever had, now has or which it or its successors hereafter can, shall or may have for, upon or by reason of any matter, cause or thing whatsoever from the beginning of the world to the day of the date of these presents. including without limitation that certain agreement by and between INTERNATIONAL BROADCASTING CORPORATION and said ELVIS PRESLEY executed on the 8th day of September, 1955 and INTERNATIONAL BROADCASTING CORPORATION does hereby further acknowledge and agree that the obligations of the said ELVIS PRESLEY under and pursuant to the said agreement were fully terminated and discharged after the performance of "Louisiana Hayride" on the 31st day of March, 1956.

This release may not be changed orally.

In Witness Whereof, *the said* INTERNATIONAL BROADCASTING CORPORATION

has caused its corporate seal to be hereunto affixed and these presents to be signed by its duly authorized officer on the 24d *day of* April, *nineteen hundred and* fifty-six

INTERNATIONAL BROADCASTING CORPORATION

(Corporate Seal)

By _H. L. Logan_____
H. L. LOGAN

LOUISIANA HAYRIDE PROGRAM DIRECTOR, HORACE LOGAN, SIGNED ELVIS PRESLEY'S BUYOUT AGREEMENT ON BEHALF OF THE INTERNATIONAL BROADCASTING CORPORATION, OWNERS OF KWKH RADIO. (TOP RIGHT) STATION MANAGER HENRY CLAY.

★ *Louisiana Hayride* ★

THE BLUE MOON BOYS

Entertainers Sunday Night . . .
Elvis Presley along with his musical side-tricks, Scotty Moore and Bill Black will appear in person, Sunday at the Slavonian Lodge Biloxi, at 8 p.m. followed with a dance in celebration of the newest air-conditioned auditorium on the Coast.

AS THE LEAD GUITARIST AND FIRST MANAGER FOR THE PRESLEY TRIO, WINFIELD SCOTT "SCOTTY" MOORE III, DID HIS BEST TO BOOK THE BAND OUT IN THE MEMPHIS AREA UNTIL BOB NEAL TOOK OVER THE POSITION. THE EARLY GIGS INCLUDED SUCH HIGH-PROFILE EVENTS AS THE DEDICATION CEREMONY FOR THE NEW AIR CONDITIONING SYSTEM AT THE SLAVONIAN LODGE.

BILL BLACK WAS THE COMEDIAN OF THE PRESLEY TRIO, OFTEN PLAYING STRAIGHT MAN TO ELVIS. KEEPING THE TEMPO FOR THE BAND WITH HIS RHYTHMIC SLAPS ON THE STAND UP BASS, BILL FREQUENTLY ADDED IN THE CLACKING SOUND OF HIS RING HITTING THE SIDE OF HIS INSTRUMENT.

LOUISIANA HAYRIDE STAFF DRUMMER DOMINICK JOSEPH "D.J." FONTANA, A NATIVE OF SHREVEPORT, BECAME A FULL-TIME MEMBER OF THE PRESLEY ENSEMBLE IN AUGUST OF 1955, ADDING A STEADY YET UNBRIDLED BEAT TO THE BAND'S GROWING REPERTOIRE OF BLUES AND ROCKABILLY MUSIC. HE REMAINED WITH ELVIS FOR THE NEXT 14 YEARS.

Louisiana Hayride

THE HAYRIDE SHOWS

Jim Ed Brown
Hayride cast member
1954-55

JIM ED BROWN

"I remember one experience in Gilmer, Texas... After the show was over, there was a piano sitting over to the side and Elvis went over to the piano while the boys were packing up everything, y'know, their guitars and all and putting them in the cars. He went over and he started playing a little and singing a little. And I noticed that people were gathering around in a big circle but they were about twelve feet away from him. They wouldn't get close to him, for some reason. I didn't know why, but that did change because soon everybody wanted to touch him. Everybody wanted to get close to him... He was a great artist..."

PRETTY GIRLS IN SEARCH OF A HUG WERE NEVER IN SHORT SUPPLY WHEN ELVIS WAS AROUND THE MUNICIPAL AUDITORIUM, SHREVEPORT - **MARCH 5, 1955.**

ELVIS AND LOUISIANA HAYRIDE PROGRAM DIRECTOR HORACE LOGAN SHARE A QUIET MOMENT
OUTSIDE THE LOCAL HIGH SCHOOL DURING A ROADSHOW IN GLADEWATER, TEXAS - **APRIL 30, 1955.**

YET ANOTHER GIRL TO HUG AT MUNICIPAL AUDITORIUM, SHREVEPORT - **AUGUST 13, 1955.**

ELVIS TOOK SECOND BILLING TO BLUEGRASS NEWCOMERS BUZZ BUSBY & THE BAYOU BOYS
WHO JOINED THE HAYRIDE CAST THAT EVENING FOR A SEVEN MONTH TENURE ON THE SHOW
- OCTOBER 1, 1955.

KWKH'S
Louisiana Hayride

Tonight
8:00 till 11:30 P.M.
MUNICIPAL AUDITORIUM

featuring:
Elvis Presley ★ Johnny Horton
Jimmy Newman
Buddy Attaway ★ Curley Herndon
Jack Ford
Jeanette Hicks ★ David Houston
Betty Amos
Buzz Busby and the Bayou Boys
and special guests
Bill Lancaster
Floyd and Loyd Armstrong
Bill Dudley
and many others

General Admission
Adults 60c   Children 30c
Reserve Section
Adults $1.00   Children 50c
Tax Included

Tickets
on Sale at
HARBUCK
& WOMACK

NOVEMBER 5, 1955

NOVEMBER 5, 1955

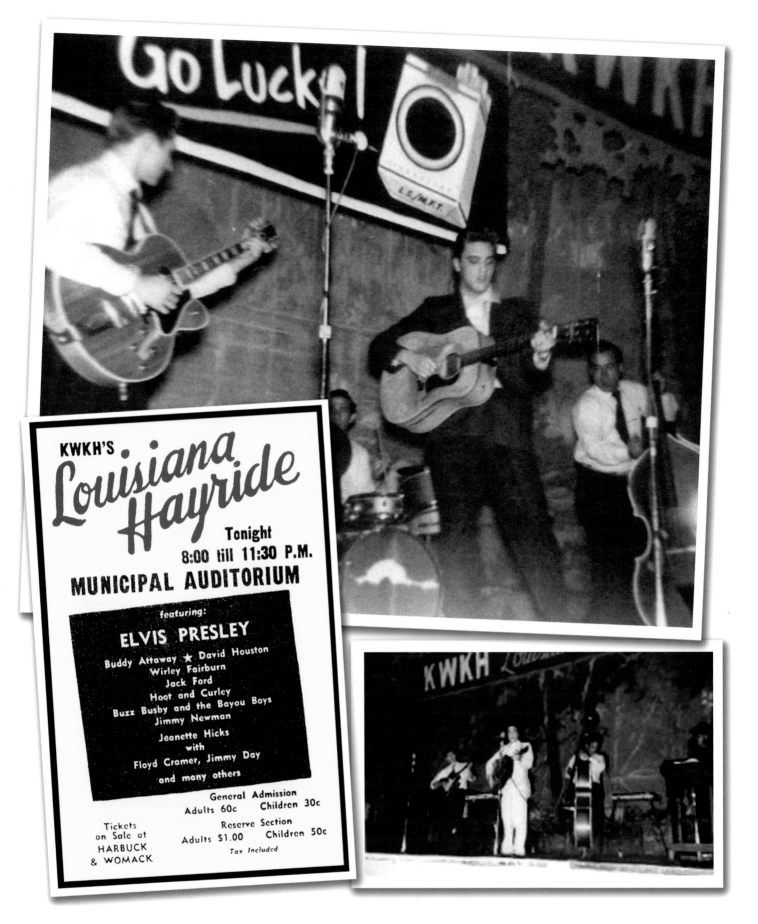

(ABOVE) AT THE HAYRIDE, MUNICIPAL AUDITORIUM IN SHREVEPORT - **NOVEMBER 12, 1955.**
(LOWER RIGHT) UNKNOWN DATE.

ELVIS THE ACCORDION PLAYER?! THE DRUMMER?! A MAN OF MANY TALENTS
- NOVEMBER 19, 1955

ELVIS ON THE HAYRIDE STAGE - **NOVEMBER 26, 1955**

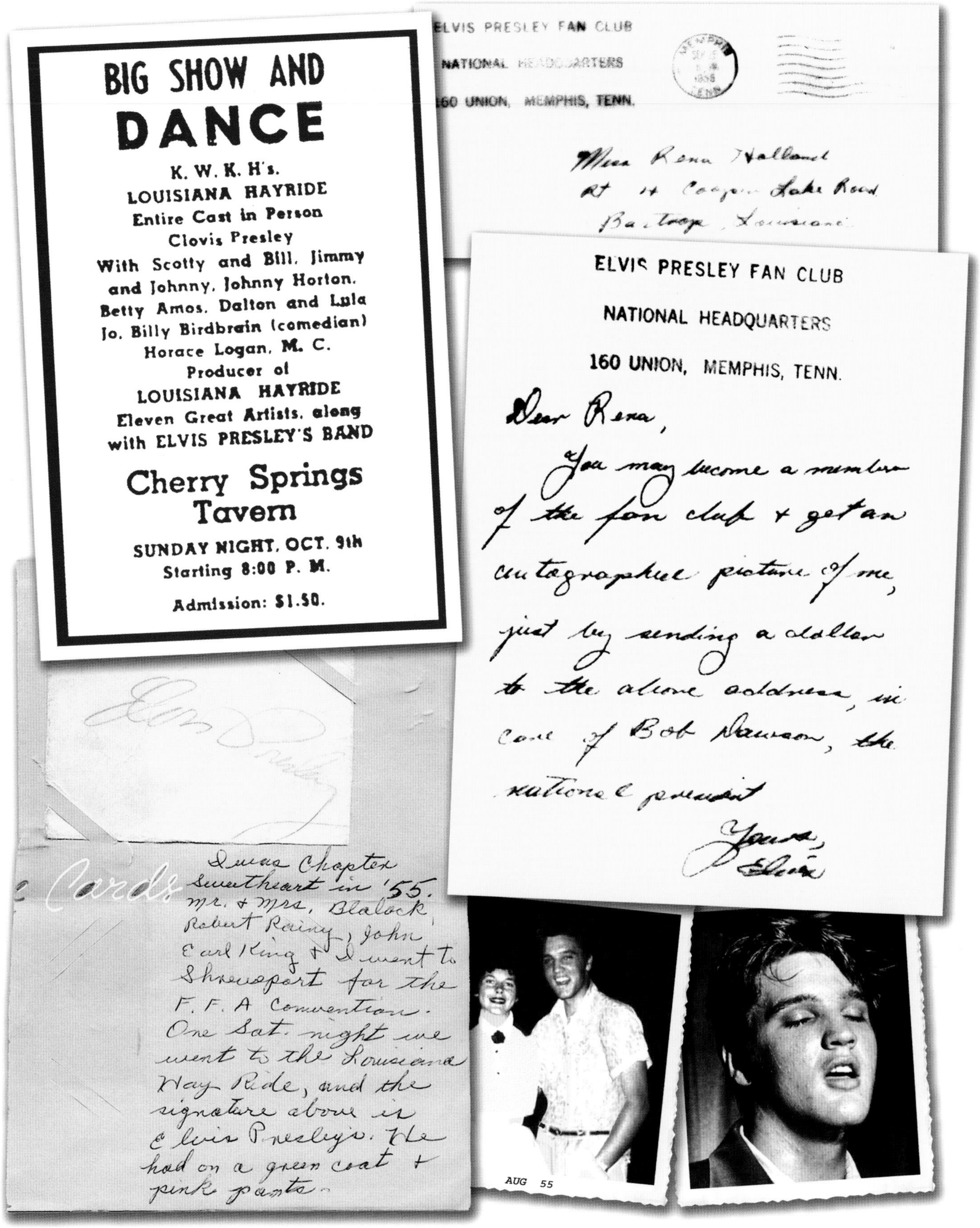
BIG SHOW AND
DANCE
K. W. K. H's.
LOUISIANA HAYRIDE
Entire Cast in Person
Clovis Presley
With Scotty and Bill, Jimmy and Johnny, Johnny Horton, Betty Amos, Dalton and Lula Jo, Billy Birdbrain (comedian)
Horace Logan, M. C.
Producer of
LOUISIANA HAYRIDE
Eleven Great Artists, along with ELVIS PRESLEY'S BAND
Cherry Springs Tavern
SUNDAY NIGHT, OCT. 9th
Starting 8:00 P. M.
Admission: $1.50.
ELVIS PRESLEY FAN CLUB
NATIONAL HEADQUARTERS
160 UNION, MEMPHIS, TENN.
Miss Rena Holland
Rt 14 Cooper Lake Road
Bastrop, Louisiana
ELVIS PRESLEY FAN CLUB
NATIONAL HEADQUARTERS
160 UNION, MEMPHIS, TENN.
Dear Rena,
You may become a member of the fan club & get an autographed picture of me, just by sending a dollar to the above address, in care of Bob Dawson, the national president
Yours,
Elvis
Cards
I was Chapter Sweetheart in '55. Mr. & Mrs. Blalock, Robert Rainy, John Earl King & I went to Shreveport for the F.F.A. Convention. One Sat. night we went to the Louisiana Hay Ride, and the signature above is Elvis Presley's. He had on a green coat + pink pants.
AUG 55

AN ASSORTMENT OF ELVIS GOODIES: AN AD FOR A LOUISIANA HAYRIDE SHOW AND DANCE FEATURING "CLOVIS" PRESLEY - **OCTOBER 7, 1955**; A PERSONAL REPLY TO A FAN LETTER FROM ELVIS - **SEPTEMBER 23, 1955**; A PHOTO WITH A FAN - **AUGUST 13, 1955**; AND A SCRAPBOOK PAGE FEATURING AN ELVIS AUTOGRAPH GATHERED ON A VISIT TO THE HAYRIDE IN 1955.

ONE OF MANY TEENAGE FANS, THIS UNKNOWN GAL GETS A HUG FROM ELVIS BACKSTAGE AT THE HAYRIDE - **DECEMBER 10, 1955**.

NORM BALE

Norm Bale
Hayride announcer
1953-71

"Everybody that came on the show while I was there was different. Elvis, of course, was the biggest difference because he came in with a brand new style. He came in with this hip shaking type of presentation that, at that time, because of the moral character of the country, people thought was vulgar. Of course, now it's as tame as could be."

ON THE CUSP OF INTERNATIONAL TELEVISION FAME, ELVIS ROCKS THE HAYRIDE BEFORE HEADING OFF TO NEW YORK FOR A SERIES OF APPEARANCES ON JIMMY & TOMMY DORSEY'S STAGE SHOW PROGRAM CARRIED BY CBS - **JANUARY 7, 1956.**

Elvis Presley

Elvis is a native of Tupelo, Mississippi, but he calls Memphis, Tennessee, his home town, having lived there most of his life. He began singing for friends and relatives when only five years old and has been at it ever since. While attending high school, he developed his unique style and gained considerable fame in and around Memphis.

Then, one day he walked into the offices of the Sun Recording Company and arranged to make a record with his friends Scotty Moore and Bill Black. The record "That's All Right" backed with "Blue Moon of Kentucky" caught on immediately and was soon being played by disc jockeys throughout the South.

As a result, Elvis was invited to make a guest appearance on the Hayride and the enthusiasm with which he was received led to his becoming a regular member of the cast in October 1954. This was followed by a tour of the South and Southwest which won for him thousands of new fans, especially among the teenage groups.

Several more recordings were released under the Sun label. These included "You're a Heartbreaker," "Milkcow Blues Boogie," "You're Right, I'm Left, She's Gone" and "Mystery Train." Presley imitators began to appear, a sure sign of success. Then he recorded "I Forgot to Remember to Forget You" and it turned the trick. It began to appear on regional popularity lists and rose rapidly to become the nation's best-selling country tune.

It was then that RCA-Victor bought Presley's contract from Sun and re-released his records under their label, along with a new disc, "Heartbreak Hotel" backed with "I Was the One." The former was the number one tune in the country music field within a few weeks and had also climbed high in the pop music lists.

Elvis has been featured on CBS-TV's "Stage Show" with Jimmy and Tommy Dorsey a number of times. He has received unprecedented attention in a number of music, radio and television magazines and is well-known from coast-to-coast. Of the many artists who have found the Hayride a springboard to fame, Elvis Presley promises to outstrip them all. Certainly his driving, belting style has brought a new era to both country and pop music and he seems well on the way to becoming one of the greatest vocal artists of all time in these fields.

ELVIS EARNED HIS VERY OWN PAGE IN THE HAYRIDE SOUVENIR PROGRAM PRINTED JUST BEFORE HE LEFT - **MARCH, 1956.**

(PAGES 84-93) THE ELVIS PRESLEY STAR WAS TRULY ON THE RISE WHEN ALL OF THESE PHOTOS WERE TAKEN DURING ONE OF HIS LAST REGULAR HAYRIDE SHOWS - **MARCH 10, 1956.**

MARCH 10, 1956

MARCH 10, 1956

ELVIS

MAR   56

MARCH 10, 1956

SLIM WHITMAN

*Slim Whitman
Hayride cast member
1950-57*

"Once when I came off stage after my act, Elvis said 'Let me wear your coat.' I told him it was way too big for him but I let him wear it. As usual, his act tore the place apart and when he came off I kidded him 'Man, the only reason you went over so big is because they all thought it was me out there in that coat'."

MARCH 10, 1956

ELVIS FAN CAROL MANGHAM GETS OUT FROM BEHIND THE CAMERA FOR HER VERY OWN PICTURE WITH THE SWEAT SOAKED KING. MUNICIPAL AUDITORIUM, SHREVEPORT - **MARCH 10, 1956.**

The Louisiana Hayride

starring
ELVIS PRESLEY

and featuring
Billy Walker
as special guest

along with the regular cast
of radio and recording
stars, including . . .

JOHNNY CASH
Jeanette Hicks • Buddy Attaway
Hoot and Curley
Buzz Busby and the Bayou Boys
Jack Ford
David Houston
and many others

MUNICIPAL AUDITORIUM
TOMORROW—8-11:30 P.M.

GENERAL ADMISSION   RESERVED SECTION
Children 30c   Adults 60c   Children 50c   Adults $1

TICKETS ON SALE AT HARBUCK & WOMACK, 304 TEXAS

ELVIS' FINAL REGULAR LOUISIANA HAYRIDE SHOW FEATURED BILLY WALKER (TOP LEFT)
AND WAS GIVEN ON **MARCH 31, 1956.**

HARRY S. STEPHENS
ATTORNEY AT LAW
HENRY C. BECK BUILDING
SHREVEPORT, LA.
TELEPHONE 3-1706

May 21, 1956

Robert Hassell Fair
3125 Parkhurst
Shreveport, Louisiana

Re: Emancipation of Robert
Hassell Fair.

Dear Robert:

I have prepared the necessary proceedings in connec-
tion with the proposed emancipation.

It will be necessary for your mother and father, both,
to sign the application for emancipation, and will also be
necessary for you to sign the same.

It is required that you be emancipated in order that
you might legally accept the sum of $200 from Elvis Presley,
by way of compromise for the injury to your jaw.

You will therefore make an appointment with me, for
your mother and father to come into the office to sign the
pledings.

Yours truly,

Harry S. Stephens

HSS/PE

HARRY S. STEPHENS
ATTORNEY AT LAW
HENRY C. BECK BUILDING
SHREVEPORT, LA.
TELEPHONE 3-1706

July 30, 1956

Mr. Benjamin Starr
1650 Broadway
New York 19, New York

Dear Mr. Starr:

Mr. Robert Hassell Fair's father has declined to
have him emancipated and states that the settlement
offered by you in the matter of altercation between
young Mr. Fair and your client, Elvis Presley, is not
a sufficient amount.

The elder Mr. Fair has, as of this date, failed
to employ me to represent him, and I therefore assume
that I am no longer interested in this matter.

Yours truly,

Harry S. Stephens

HSS/pj

CC Milton Wade Fair

Louisiana Hayride
Program Director
Horace Logan

HAYRIDE ANNOUNCER HORACE LOGAN RECALLED A LITTLE SCUFFLE ELVIS
GOT INTO BACKSTAGE ONE NIGHT EARLY IN 1956.

"The non-stop grind was starting to take a noticeable toll... One night one of the helpers backstage bumped into Elvis as he was getting ready to go on. Almost like a reflex, Elvis whirled around, smacked the guy on the jaw and knocked him flat on the floor. The stagehand was sprawled there on the seat of his pants when Elvis realized what he'd done. I've never seen anybody turn so contrite in such a hurry. The next thing I knew, Elvis was down on the floor beside the guy apologizing and trying to help him up. 'God, I'm sorry,' he said. 'I-I don't know what got into me, man. Are you hurt?' The guy finally got up, but he wasn't too steady on his feet. He leaned against the wall and mumbled something I couldn't hear. 'I'm really sorry,' Elvis said again. 'Hey, hang on. I'll get somebody to call a doctor.' 'Nah, I'm all right,' the guy said. 'You sure?' 'Yeah, I'll be okay.' Elvis was still white as a sheet when he walked out on the stage a minute later for his first song."

APR 56

APR 56

APR 56

AFTER HE LEFT THE HAYRIDE, ELVIS CONTINUED TO PLAY DATES THROUGHOUT THE SOUTHWEST LIKE THE MUNICIPAL AUDITORIUM IN AMARILLO, TEXAS ON **APRIL 13, 1956.**

IN SAN ANTONIO, AN ARTICLE CALLED "WHAT MAKES ELVIS TICK" SENDS ELVIS LOOKING FOR THE CROSSWORD PUZZLE INSTEAD - **OCTOBER 14, 1956.**

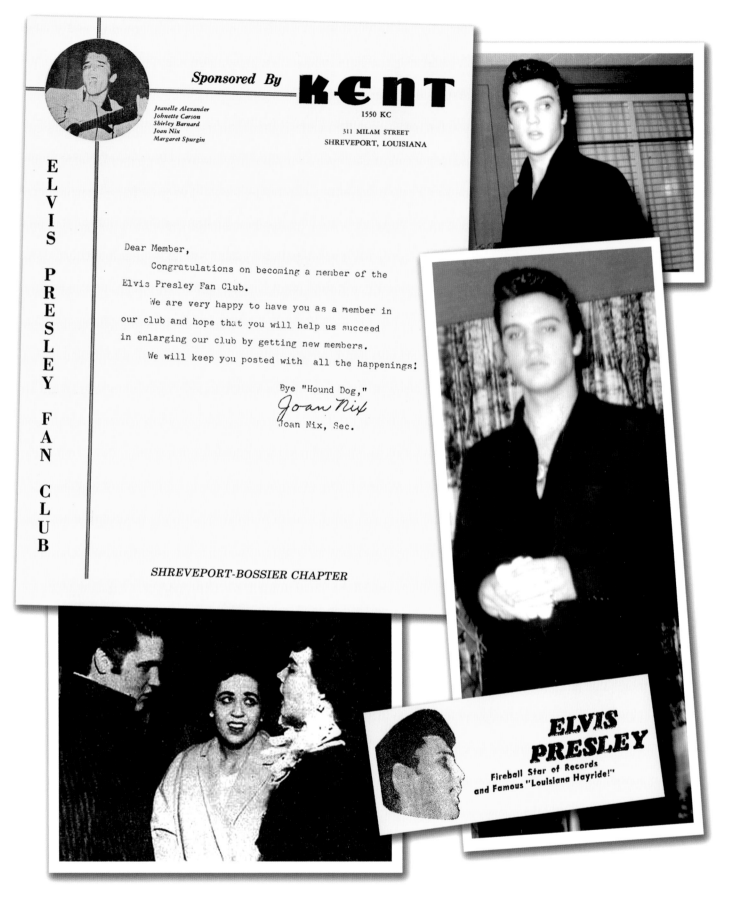

Sponsored By **KENT**

1550 KC

311 MILAM STREET
SHREVEPORT, LOUISIANA

Jeanelle Alexander
Johnette Carson
Shirley Barnard
Joan Nix
Margaret Spurgin

ELVIS PRESLEY FAN CLUB

Dear Member,

Congratulations on becoming a member of the
Elvis Presley Fan Club.

We are very happy to have you as a member in
our club and hope that you will help us succeed
in enlarging our club by getting new members.

We will keep you posted with all the happenings!

Bye "Hound Dog,"

Joan Nix

Joan Nix, Sec.

SHREVEPORT-BOSSIER CHAPTER

ELVIS PRESLEY

Fireball Star of Records
and Famous "Louisiana Hayride!"

THE FIRST ELVIS PRESLEY FAN CLUB OUTSIDE OF MEMPHIS WAS FORMED IN SHREVEPORT. SPONSORED BY LOCAL RADIO STATION, KENT, THE CLUB THRIVED UNDER ITS' PRESIDENT, JEANELLE ALEXANDER. JEANELLE VENTURED TO MEMPHIS IN APRIL OF 1957 AND TOOK SEVERAL CANDID SHOTS OF ELVIS AT HIS HOME ON AUDUBON DRIVE JUST BEFORE HE MOVED TO GRACELAND. THE CLUB HELD SPECIAL EVENTS LIKE AN ADVANCE SCREENING OF "LOVE ME TENDER" IN **NOVEMBER, 1956.**

RONNIE McDOWELL

Ronnie McDowell
Elvis impersonator
1977 to present

"One day my sisters brought an Elvis Presley record home and they kinda mixed it in with Little Richard and all this, and to me, it sounded like the same kind of music but there was something different about it. And I never will forget the day they brought in Hound Dog. When I first heard that, it was like I got down and played that over and over and over and over and over. And when I first heard it, it was like somebody took a bucket of water and just poured it all over me. It was like 'Woah! I've never heard anything like this!'... I don't know, I guess, Elvis reached and touched me like he did everybody else around the world."

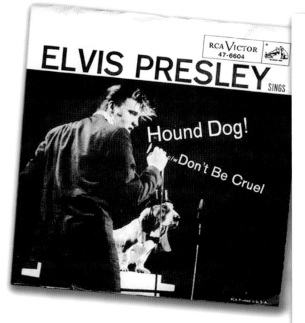

★ Louisiana Hayride ★

THE FINAL HAYRIDE

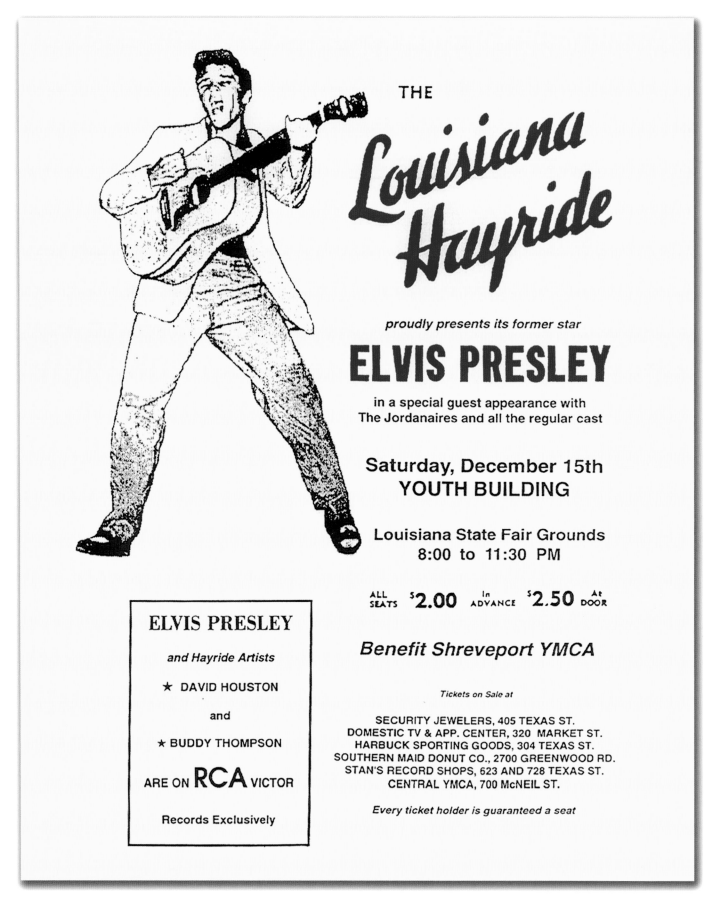

THE

Louisiana Hayride

proudly presents its former star

ELVIS PRESLEY

in a special guest appearance with
The Jordanaires and all the regular cast

Saturday, December 15th
YOUTH BUILDING

Louisiana State Fair Grounds
8:00 to 11:30 PM

ALL SEATS $2.00 In ADVANCE $2.50 At DOOR

Benefit Shreveport YMCA

Tickets on Sale at

SECURITY JEWELERS, 405 TEXAS ST.
DOMESTIC TV & APP. CENTER, 320 MARKET ST.
HARBUCK SPORTING GOODS, 304 TEXAS ST.
SOUTHERN MAID DONUT CO., 2700 GREENWOOD RD.
STAN'S RECORD SHOPS, 623 AND 728 TEXAS ST.
CENTRAL YMCA, 700 McNEIL ST.

Every ticket holder is guaranteed a seat

ELVIS PRESLEY

and Hayride Artists

★ DAVID HOUSTON

and

★ BUDDY THOMPSON

ARE ON **RCA** VICTOR

Records Exclusively

SHREVEPORT TIMES AD FOR ELVIS PRESLEY'S FINAL LOUISIANA HAYRIDE APPEARANCE - **DECEMBER 15, 1956.**

ON WITH THE SHOW

By PERICLES ALEXANDER

The Presley Phenomenon

The most controversial figure of this entertainment day and age will sashay into Greater Shreveport Saturday for a YMCA-benefit performance on KWKH's "Louisiana Hayride," or haven't you heard?

He is Elvis Presley, who has parlayed a guitar, an untrained voice, and a wriggle that puts Marilyn Monroe's wiggle to shame, into a million-dollar jackpot for himself and Col. Tom Parker.

Quite frankly, we have cause to admire the 21-year-old, Valentino side-burned youth and wish we had as much "no talent" to be in his income tax bracket. In presleyism there is no middle ground. You either think that he is super sensational and "the most" or strictly no talent."

Let's face it. The kid's got something, including an enviable bank balance and a different Caddy to ride in every day of the week if he doesn't have a yen to go joy-riding on his motorcycle.

Show business needed a Presley as much as movies needed Marilyn to bring audiences to rapt attention once again.

In Elvis' spiraling to fame and fortune, Radio Station KWKH and the "Louisiana Hayride" played a part even as they did in the careers of Slim Whitman, Webb Pierce, and the late Hank Williams.

The swivel-hipped singer's entry into the bigtime is dated from his appearance on the Milton Berle Show last mid-summer. For some months prior to that, however, Elvis had been a rising performer, he had made deep inroads on disc sales and was a hit in his personal appearances.

For most of 1956, Presley has been way out front in the disc business with a near 1,000,000 advance sale on his "Love Me Tender" for RCA-Victor and he registered solidly at the movie box offices in his debut picture by the same name. Although the average teen-ager is not in the market for a class automobile, Car Salesman Ed Sullivan did an about face and snapped up Elvis for a series of appearances on his Sunday night TV clambake.

Elvis is the unquestioned idol of the American teen-ager and Presley merchandise beamed at the teen-age crowd as inevitable. The Presley campaign with merchandise ranging from book-ends and bracelets to wallets is unprecedented in that it represents the first all-out merchandising drive aimed at teen-agers.

Other promotions ("Hopalong Cassidy," "Davy Crockett," Gene Autry, and Roy Rogers) were on the children's level with mom and dad having to shell out the cash. Some half a hundred Presley items are on the market mainly for the female teen-ager.

New Presley merchandising gimmicks can be expected in 1957. Deals are being negotiated for Presley "Hound Dogs" (a large hotdog) and Presley "Houndburghers" (a "hamburger with glamour").

All this on an adding machine adds up to big business and in the year drawing to a close the Presley gross is estimated at $1,000,000.

Shortly after his appearance here Saturday night, Presley will return to Hollywood to make a western movie for Hal Wallis, an astute producer who has another Ark-La-Texan, Earl Holliman, who doesn't have a git-tar to his name, under longterm contract.

One has to take off his hat and bow low to Elvis. He has given the nation's columnists, editorial writers, psychologists, teachers, teen-agers, adults, clerics, and show business something to cuss and discuss between TV programs and world crises.

We doubt that all this scarcely fazes the Presley boy just so everybody spells his name right—E-L-V-I-S P-R-E-S-L-E-Y. He's not a fad. He's a phenomenon of today's world.

Elvis really loved Shreveport and put on one of his best shows ever during the winter of 1956. It was held in the largest facility in the city, the Hirsch Youth Building at the State Fair Grounds. Tickets were $2.00 in advance and $2.50 at the door. The proceeds went to benefit the YMCA Camp just south of Shreveport, and were used to build, among other things, a swimming pool.

The date was December 15, 1956. The yellow Caddy limousine pulled in from Memphis at five a.m., and a weary Elvis checked into the Captain Shreve Hotel in downtown Shreveport. It was hard to imagine this was the place, barely two years earlier he'd sat with Scotty and Bill and Sam Phillips, and dreamed of leaving truck driving for a career in music. Now, Elvis found himself longing for a simpler life, for just a little peace and quiet. He opened the window of his room and shouted down a plea for quiet to the crowd already forming below so he could get some much needed sleep.

THE CAPTAIN SHREVE HOTEL IN DOWNTOWN SHREVEPORT CIRCA 1956.

ELVIS   103

Failing in their mission to keep the location of his hotel room secret, the police turned their attention to the upcoming concert. A plot was hatched to set up a fake Elvis to decoy the avid fans away from the real one. Patrolman Robert Catts had the same build and sleepy eyes so he was awarded (or punished, depending on how you look at it) with the task of impersonating the King.

Officer Catts was outfitted in Elvis attire and a pink Cadillac was even brought in from a local car dealer to complete the ruse. At the appointed hour, the Caddy took off with a police escort for the five mile journey to the state fairgrounds. When the motorcade pulled up to the entrance of the Youth Building, Catts and his entourage were mobbed while the real Elvis slipped quietly in the back door almost unnoticed.

It had been just over two years since Elvis had first appeared on the stage of the Louisiana Hayride. The seating capacity of the Youth Building was right at 10,000 and every ticket had been sold. We'd tried to keep the fire marshal happy by setting up a fence in front of the stage and limiting the number of chairs on the floor of the coliseum, but as soon as the doors were opened, that plan went out the window. A solid mass of teenagers grabbed at the chairs and drug them as close to the stage as possible.

Horace Logan remembers: "As far as the fire marshal was concerned, there wasn't going to be a Hayride show that night if something wasn't done - and fast! We'd found out an hour or so before the show that some local polio patients in iron lungs would be attending the performance, so I got on the stage microphone and announced we had to clear an area down front for their gurneys. The kids seemed to understand that these iron lung patients, many of them kids themselves, wouldn't be able to see the show otherwise. In a few minutes, the necessary buffer zone was established and the attendants got the patients in position right in front of the stage and the show was allowed to proceed... almost on time."

The two primary local newspapers, The Shreveport Times and The Shreveport Journal, dispatched their top photographers to cover the mayhem. Langston McEachern shot for the Times and Jack Barham for the Journal. The two were given unlimited access to the facility and moved about freely on stage and off.

I had been with Elvis every Saturday night he'd performed on the Hayride and knew how audiences had come to react to this young man. I was prepared for something bigger than that, but I wasn't prepared for that evening. When Elvis finally came on stage, thousands of Brownie Reflex cameras went off simultaneously. Several of the photographs taken that night show me off to one side and I look terrified. I was! I had never heard ten thousand teenagers screaming at the top of their lungs before. It was absolutely frightening. The screaming began when Elvis came out on stage and it never let up for the entire time he performed. Many people told me later that the audience couldn't tell whether he was singing or not, or even if the band was playing... and nobody cared. The King had come home.

Masquerading as Elvis Fun, but Scary

By CRAIG FLOURNOY
Journal Staff Writer

It was a once-in-a-lifetime offer — to masquerade as Elvis Presley for one night. Not at some dumb masquerade ball but at a live Elvis-concert.

Just think — the girls, thousands of 'em, literally fighting to touch you as you sit impersonating Him, the King of Rock n' Roll, in a big pink Cadillac with a police escort showing just how important the whole occasion is.

It was a hell of a heady offer for young Shreveport Ptn. Robert Catts. It was the day of Dec. 15, 1956, and Elvis was returning to Shreveport for the first time since he'd left the Louisiana Hayride.

It was the afternoon of Elvis' concert return and Catts had just been called into the office of Capt. Felix Porter, boss of the patrol division's evening shift. Capt. Porter explained his problem: Elvis would be mobbed by thousands of young girls when he arrived at Hirsch Memorial Coliseum for his concert appearance. A decoy was needed to draw the crowd's attention so that Elvis could slip in the back entrance. Was Catts interested?

"I was all for it," remembered Catts, now a lieutenant in the city's traffic engineering division.

Why was he selected? Catts said it was because he very much physically resembled Elvis then with the long black hair combed back, the lanky build and, not to be forgotten, "the droopy eyes."

Clothes had to be secured. Since Catts would remain in an automobile during the charade, his powder blue patrol trousers would suffice. What needed snazzing up was the upper half of his body. It was decided he would wear a white silk shirt along with a sportscoat that Catts could only describe as "loud" in color. Of course, the sportcoat's collar would be turned up, a traditional Elvis touch.

The hour of Elvis' appearance drew closer. But still, one more item of importance was needed — a pink Cadillac, another Elvis trademark. Capt. Porter managed to borrow one from a local garage and the masquerade — admittedly a rush job — was complete.

Decked out in his fancy attire and a police car serving as his escort, "Elvis" (a.k.a. Catts) headed out for his date with destiny. Capt. Porter was the driver of the big Caddy while then-Ptn. James Hood was bodyguard for the charade.

Carloads of girls spotted the entourage on its way to the coliseum and before long a long line of cars trailed the false Elvis. Catts remembered the hand-waving, the kisses blown his way and admitted it felt good to be such a hot commodity.

Soon the masquerading show reached the grounds of the State Fair complex just minutes before the real Elvis was scheduled to arrive. As it approached Hirsch, a crowd of 5,000 to 6,000 young people, mostly girls, lay in wait. The stage was set.

The escort police car turned on its red lights to draw the crowd's attention and "then they started coming," today's Catts almost gulped.

In a matter of seconds, girls were everywhere, jumping on the Cadillac, screaming and clawing to get at "Elvis." Unknown to the mob, Capt. Porter radioed another police car carrying the real Elvis that the decoy had worked. As the excitement and screams built up in front of Hirsch, Elvis, the Real Elvis, was quietly dropped off at a rear entrance.

But what had it been like, to be Elvis Presley, even if it only lasted a few minutes? "The first time I enjoyed it. I liked the girls," Catts, a married man then and now, admitted somewhat sheepishly.

But then he gravely added: "The mob at the Coliseum scared me. I knew then I didn't want to be Elvis, not what he went through. I could just picture him — always being grabbed at, always having to hide, not being able to live a normal life. But that's the price of fame . . . I guess."

* * *

Almost 20 years later, Elvis returned to Shreveport in July, 1976 for what would be his last concert here. He set up temporary residence at the Chateau Motor Inn, using the entire fourth floor for

Lt. Robert Catts; Elvis Presley lookalike, 21 years later.

lodging. Three policemen were needed to help with security and Elvis, remembering the charade of 20 years ago, specifically requested that Robert Catts be one of those three.

No masquerade was planned for this concert. After it was over, Elvis returned to his room to engage in something Catts said Elvis regularly practiced: reading the Bible. "He was a man of the Lord," Catts said. "He always kept his Bible with him."

While reading his Bible, Elvis looked up and thought he saw something rather strange in his room. Catts, who was watching him, said Elvis at first pretended to shake it off, then did a double-take and shot out of the room.

The reason? A de-scented skunk, placed in Elvis' room by one of the police officers at the request of Sonny West, one of Elvis' bodyguards.

But Elvis took the practical joke good-naturedly, Catts remembered. "He just laughed and came over to the security room to talk to us."

Over in the security room, Elvis talked of his respect for police officers, of his liking for Shreveport and of his appreciation for the masquerade stunt pulled off at his concert 20 years ago, Catts said.

How much had Elvis changed since 1956? "He had gained some weight but he still had that same Elvis look," Catts replied.

Catts also discounted reports that Elvis was using drugs heavily. "He did not look like he was using drugs," Catts said, adding that one bodyguard told him Elvis once fired a band member for using marijuana.

But what about Elvis the man, the person apart from the superstar image? "He always seemed like he was considerate and very gentle like he had never made it big." Catts remembered Elvis saying he wanted to get out and see more of Shreveport during his short stay but that he couldn't because of his vast popularity.

"You know," Catts said, "he looked like he just wanted to get out (of the superstar's life) but couldn't. Just be almost a common person."

But would he have liked to be Elvis? "I would rather be Robert Catts than Elvis Presley. I'm 45 and I'm still alive."

HIRSCH COLISEUM

(ABOVE) A 1977 SHREVEPORT JOURNAL ARTICLE TELLS PATROLMAN ROBERT CATTS' STORY IN HIS OWN WORDS.

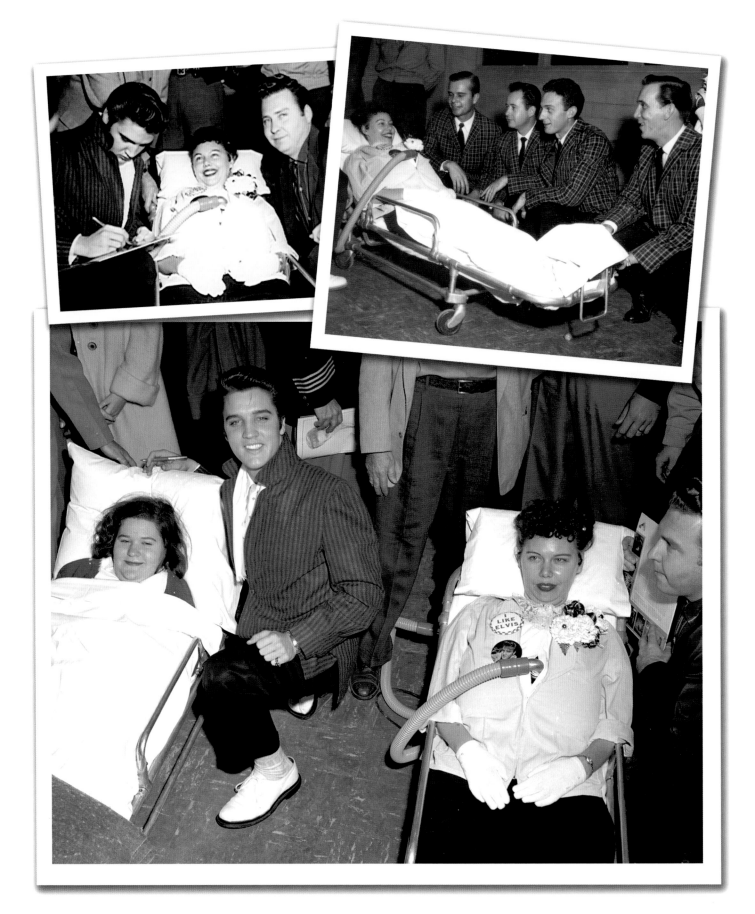

POLIO PATIENT BETTY FIELDS GETS ALL THE ATTENTION FROM ELVIS AND HIS BACKUP SINGERS, THE JORDANAIRES, DURING HIS FINAL HAYRIDE APPEARANCE. BETTY WAS THE WINNER IN A CONTEST SPONSORED BY LOCAL RADIO STATION, KENT.

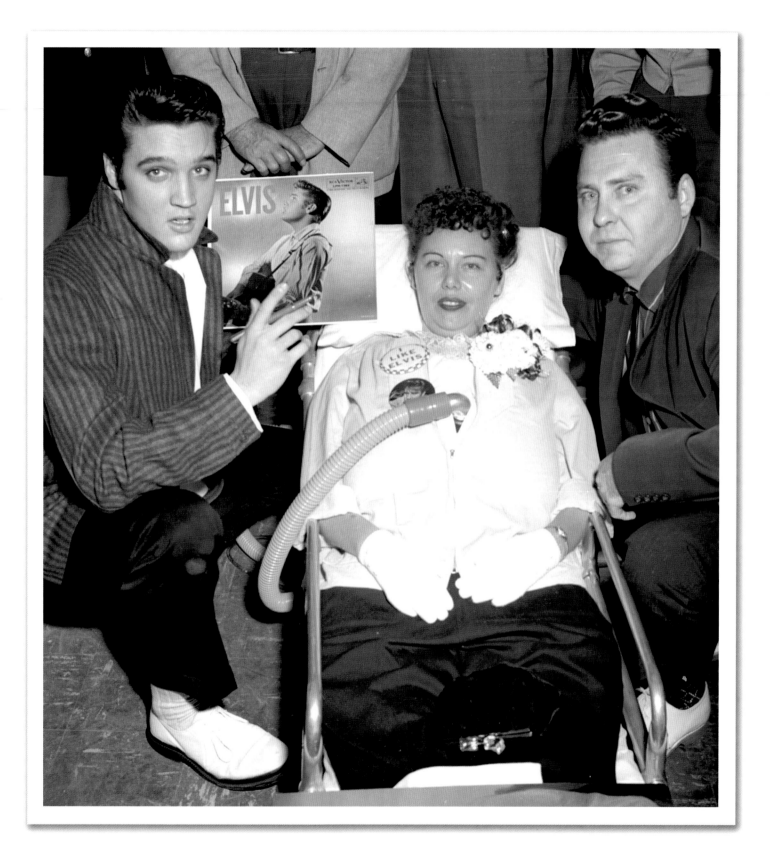

In addition to his duties for the Journal, Jack Barham was on assignment for Life Magazine. Life was preparing a story about Elvis and needed a photo to illustrate a conversation between Presley and his Japanese counterpart. Yes, there were Elvis impersonators even back then! Backstage was "organized chaos" at best and Jack found Elvis and Colonel Tom Parker in a small room amid a sea of media, fans, promoters and Hayride performers. Jack explained to the Colonel the need to "stage" a shot of Elvis on the phone to illustrate the conversation that had already taken place between the two nationals. The Colonel seized upon the excuse to clear the room and give his star some quiet time before the performance.

The dressing room had one standard rotary phone with a six-foot cord on a shelf in the corner. The cramped quarters quickly proved unyielding as Jack searched in vain for a good angle and the Colonel grew impatient.

The Colonel, however, was not to be defeated. He quickly provided his own solution by yanking the phone from the wall and bellowing at Jack and Elvis to follow him into the hall. A folding chair was plopped down and Elvis was ordered to talk on the phone whose shredded wires dangled out of frame. Jack sat Elvis in the chair backwards for a casual feeling and the photo shoot was over in short order.

Elvis retreated back inside the dressing room and invited Jack to keep him company while he warmed up for the show. Not one to waste the moment, the Colonel grabbed Langston and talked him into shooting his wheeler-dealer self "working the phones" from a squatting position. Hokey? Yes, but that was Colonel Tom Parker. Elvis took the stage about half-past nine that evening.

He was part of a regular Hayride show but we knew we couldn't contain the audience much longer. His 35-minute performance included ten songs: "Heartbreak Hotel", "Long Tall Sally", "I Was The One", "Love Me Tender", "Don't Be Cruel", "Love Me", "I Got A Woman", "When My Blue Moon Turns To Gold Again", "Paralyzed", and "Hound Dog."

"I Was The One," a ballad Elvis was most proud of and his personal favorite from his first RCA session, was followed with "Love Me Tender," the theme from the motion picture, he tells the audience, "in which I got blasted." Backing Elvis that evening was the popular gospel group "The Jordanaires" who would tour and record with him for many years to come.

Langston and Jack swirled around the entertainer, trying to capture some of his tremendous energy on film. Both snapped pictures furiously and did their best with the existing lighting conditions. Neither really sensed the lasting impact this kid would have on the music scene. None of us did. He was just our friend Elvis and this was, for us, just one more night on the job. With that in mind, Langston broke free and rushed off to make the deadline for the Times. Jack stayed behind to finish up. Elvis in his green sport coat and the Jordanaires in matching

ELVIS AND HIS BACKUP SINGERS,
"THE VERY WONDERFUL JORDANAIRES"
DECEMBER 15, 1956

Frenzied Elvis Fans Rock Youth Center

plaid continued to work the audience to a fever pitch. Perhaps the most potent stick of audio dynamite in the Louisiana Hayride archives is Elvis' encore performance of "Hound Dog" from that evening.

Nowhere is it more evident the change he has undergone in the span of two short years than the drawn out "burlesque" rendition he gave of that popular hit.

Record and movie executives looked on from the wings and were dumbfounded. They had been forewarned, but comparisons to a young Frank Sinatra would no longer paint the picture of the power Elvis had and the frenzy his presence could evoke. This was something new... something entirely different. At last, the world was ready for Elvis Presley.

THE REAL ELVIS "TALKS" TO A JAPANESE ELVIS IMPERSONATOR DURING THIS STAGED PHOTO FOR LIFE MAGAZINE TAKEN BY SHREVEPORT JOURNAL PHOTOGRAPHER, JACK BARHAM, BACKSTAGE AT THE HIRSCH YOUTH BUILDING IN SHREVEPORT.

"COLONEL" TOM PARKER TRIES TO LOOK IMPORTANT BACKSTAGE DURING ELVIS' FINAL HAYRIDE PERFORMANCE.

BY THE TIME HIS FINAL HAYRIDE DATE ROLLED AROUND, THE PRESLEY SNARL HAD BEEN PERFECTED.

Louisiana Hayride

★ ★

AN UNFORGETTABLE PERFORMANCE

MAXINE BROWN

Maxine Brown
Hayride cast member
1954-55

"We were all having dinner one night after our show and getting ready for a long haul to the next big gig when Ferlin [Huskey] asked our waitress 'What kind of soup do you have?' She said, 'Well, we have tomato, mushroom, chicken and pea soup.' Ferlin ordered chicken soup. As the waitress walked off, he stood up and hollered as loud as he could, 'Hold that chicken and make it pea.' Everyone died laughing. I thought Elvis was going to crack a rib he laughed so hard."

(RIGHT) ELVIS SITS WITH THE BROWN SISTERS AT A DINER IN PINE BLUFF, ARKANSAS EN ROUTE TO HIS FINAL HAYRIDE SHOW.

AMONG THE PROFESSIONAL PHOTOGRAPHERS COVERING ELVIS' FINAL HAYRIDE APPEARANCE WERE (CLOCKWISE FROM TOP LEFT): J. FRANK McANENY, JACK BARHAM, C. G. GRAHAM, LLOYD STILLEY AND LANGSTON McEACHERN.

(LEFT) BELMORE HICKS OF THE SHREVEPORT TIMES HELPED DECORATE ELVIS' DRESSING ROOM WITH A FLOCKED CHRISTMAS TREE. HER EFFORTS WERE REWARDED WITH A VISIT WITH THE KING BEFORE THE SHOW (ABOVE).

KWKH STATION MANAGER HENRY CLAY (ABOVE LEFT) WAS ON HAND FOR ELVIS' FINAL HAYRIDE SHOW, WHERE HIS CHILDREN, GINNY & HELEN, AND THEIR FRIENDS WERE TREATED TO A SPECIAL PHOTO OPPORTUNITY WITH THE STAR OF THE EVENING.

SHREVEPORT RECORD SHOP OWNER AND DISTRIBUTOR, STAN LEWIS, AND HIS WIFE, PAULINE, POSE WITH THEIR LONGTIME FRIEND ELVIS PRESLEY FOR ONE FINAL PHOTO AT THE HIRSCH YOUTH BUILDING, SHREVEPORT - **DECEMBER 15, 1956.**

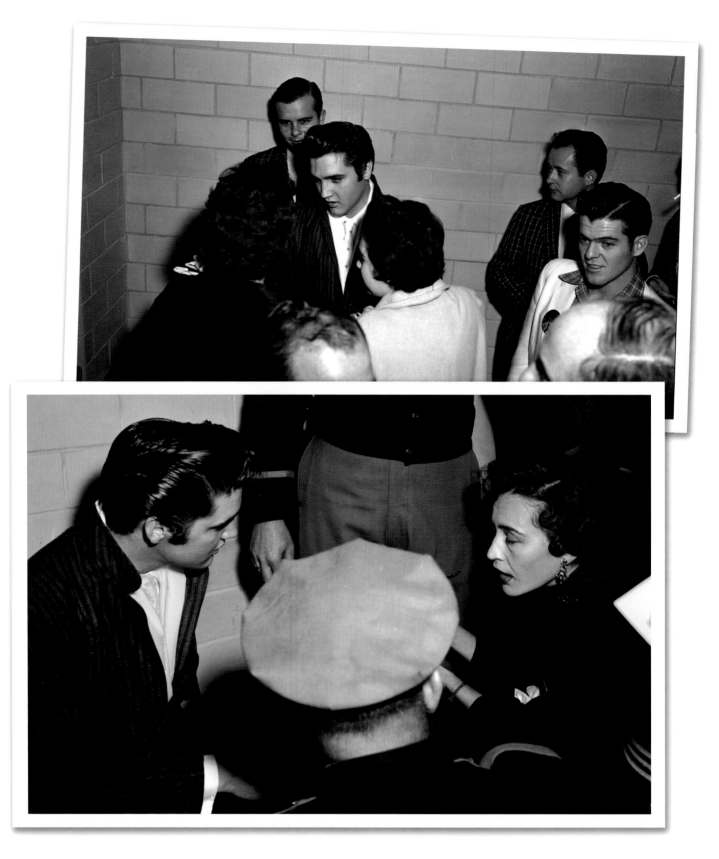

ELVIS CHATS WITH VARIOUS FAN CLUB OFFICERS AND REPORTERS BACKSTAGE AT THE HIRSCH YOUTH BUILDING BEFORE THE BIG SHOW IN SHREVEPORT - **DECEMBER 15, 1956.**

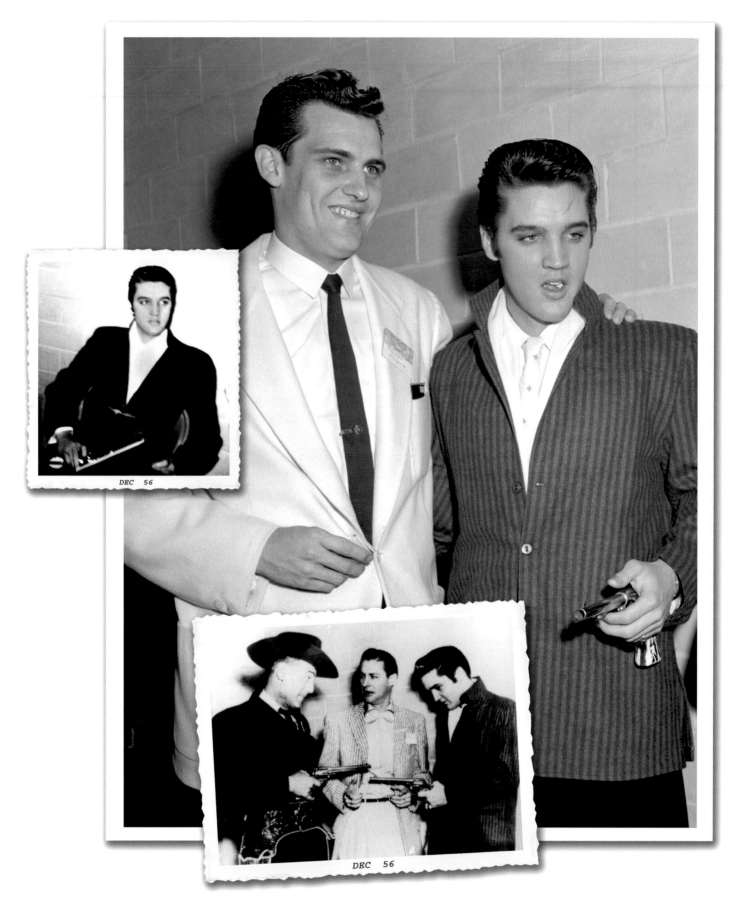

ELVIS OFTEN ADMIRED THE SET OF SIX GUNS WORN BY HAYRIDE PROGRAM DIRECTOR HORACE LOGAN. A GIFT FROM HAYRIDE STAR WEBB PIERCE, THE GUNS WERE A PRIZED POSSESSION OF LOGAN'S WHO WAS, HIMSELF, A SKILLED GUNSMITH. (ABOVE) DISC JOCKEY ED HAMILTON BREAKS UP THE FEUD BETWEEN TWO GOOD FRIENDS, AND ELVIS STRIKES A POSE WITH HIS FIRST HAYRIDE BUDDY, MERLE KILGORE.

ELVIS SELECTED A GOSPEL QUARTET KNOWN AS "THE JORDANAIRES" TO BACK HIM DURING HIS FINAL HAYRIDE PERFORMANCE. THE GROUP WOULD STICK WITH ELVIS FOR MANY YEARS TO COME, APPEARING WITH HIM IN PERSON AND SINGING ON HIS RECORDS. (ABOVE) THE JORDANAIRES ARE THE FIRST TO BE CORNERED BY THE SWARM OF REPORTERS ON HAND FOR THE SHOW...

...AND THE FIRST REPORTER TO FIND ELVIS WAS SHREVEPORT DISC JOCKEY AND FELLOW HAYRIDE ARTIST, VAN GIVENS (ABOVE), KNOWN TO ROCKABILLY FANS AS TOMMY BLAKE. TOMMY BLAKE & HIS REBELS WOULD HAVE A CHART RECORD OF THEIR OWN, "FLATFOOT SAM," IN THE YEAR FOLLOWING THE DEPARTURE OF ELVIS FROM THE HAYRIDE.

TIME FOR A COUPLE OF QUICK PROMOTIONAL PHOTOS, AND THEN "ON WITH THE SHOW!"
PAY ATTENTION, ELVIS...

THAT'S BETTER!

Elvis Due To Gyrate Here Today

The Ark-La-Tex and Shreveport is set to rock 'n' roll today with the leading exponent of the fad.

Gyrating troubadour Elvis Presley will undulate into Shreveport from his home in Memphis to headline KWKH's "Louisiana Hayride" in a special benefit performance at 8 p.m. at the Youth Building on the Louisiana State Fair Grounds. It will mark the Pelvis' first appearance on the "Hayride" since he hit the big time.

Before his wriggling style of song delivery catapulted him into national prominence, Presley had made several appearances on the KWKH show.

At a late hour last night details of Elvis' arrival from Memphis, including the hour, were top secret. A radio and press conference has been set up for the rock 'n' roller but it will be held tonight at the Youth Building before he starts the big arena to rocking and rolling.

Elvis will be supported and surrounded tonight by the regular line-up of "Hayride artists, plus the Jordanaires. Capital Recording stars from Nashville, Tenn.

All proceeds from tonight's benefit performance will go to the Shreveport YMCA

DEC 56

READY FOR THE STAGE, ELVIS TAKES A MOMENT TO REVIEW THE GIANT POSTER MADE BY "TRUE PRESLEY FAN," SUE HOLSTROM.

"LET'S GET WITH IT!"

KWKH LOUISIANA HAYRIDE
with special guest star
ELVIS PRESLEY

Youth Building, Louisiana State Fair Grounds
Shreveport, Saturday, Dec. 15th - 8:00 p.m.

★   Benefit Shreveport YMCA

PRESS and RADIO

(ABOVE) A PRESS AND RADIO PASS FOR THE BIG EVENT. TICKET PRICES WERE $2.00 IN ADVANCE, $2.50 AT THE DOOR!

DECEMBER 15, 1956

DECEMBER 15, 1956

DECEMBER 15, 1956

DECEMBER 15, 1956

DECEMBER 15, 1956

DECEMBER 15, 1956

DECEMBER 15, 1956

DECEMBER 15, 1956

DECEMBER 15, 1956

DECEMBER 15, 1956

DEC 56

DEC 56

DECEMBER 15, 1956

DECEMBER 15, 1956

DECEMBER 15, 1956

DECEMBER 15, 1956

DECEMBER 15, 1956

DECEMBER 15, 1956

DECEMBER 15, 1956

DECEMBER 15, 1956

DECEMBER 15, 1956

DECEMBER 15, 1956

DECEMBER 15, 1956

DECEMBER 15, 1956

DECEMBER 15, 1956

DECEMBER 15, 1956

DISC JOCKEY PAUL KELLINGER INTERVIEWS ELVIS AFTER THE SHOW AS HAYRIDE STAR JOHNNY HORTON LOOKS ON.

A FEW MORE CANDID SHOTS OF ELVIS FROM HIS DAYS ON THE LOUISIANA HAYRIDE.

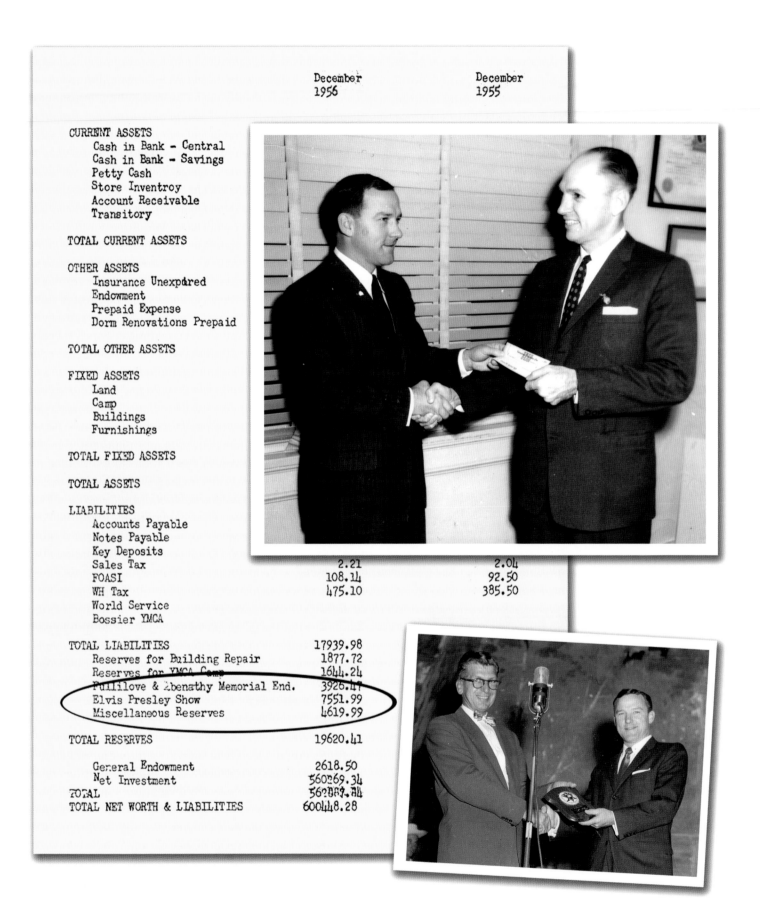

	December 1956	December 1955
CURRENT ASSETS		
Cash in Bank - Central		
Cash in Bank - Savings		
Petty Cash		
Store Inventroy		
Account Receivable		
Transitory		
TOTAL CURRENT ASSETS		
OTHER ASSETS		
Insurance Unexpired		
Endowment		
Prepaid Expense		
Dorm Renovations Prepaid		
TOTAL OTHER ASSETS		
FIXED ASSETS		
Land		
Camp		
Buildings		
Furnishings		
TOTAL FIXED ASSETS		
TOTAL ASSETS		
LIABILITIES		
Accounts Payable		
Notes Payable		
Key Deposits		
Sales Tax	2.21	2.04
FOASI	108.14	92.50
WH Tax	475.10	385.50
World Service		
Bossier YMCA		
TOTAL LIABILITIES	17939.98	
Reserves for Building Repair	1877.72	
Reserves for YMCA Camp	1644.24	
Pullilove & Abenathy Memorial End.	3926.47	
Elvis Presley Show	7551.99	
Miscellaneous Reserves	4619.99	
TOTAL RESERVES	19620.41	
General Endowment	2618.50	
Net Investment	560269.34	
TOTAL	562887.84	
TOTAL NET WORTH & LIABILITIES	600448.28	

(TOP LEFT) KWKH GENERAL MANAGER HENRY CLAY, CHAIRMAN OF THE SHREVEPORT YMCA'S BUILDING & EXPANSION PROGRAM FOR 1956, PRESENTS A CHECK TO THE "Y" FOR $7,551.99 REPRESENTING THE NET PROCEEDS FROM ELVIS'S FINAL HAYRIDE SHOW. IN TURN, CLAY RECEIVED A PLAQUE FROM THE "Y" FOR HELPING REACH THEIR FINANCIAL GOALS FOR THE YEAR.

GARY BRYANT

Gary Bryant
Hayride cast member
1956-57

"For that last appearance he made on the Hayride, when he left and came back months later, no one wanted to follow him. They took the show out to the fairgrounds and none of the other acts wanted to face his fans after he left. So, I said 'I'll do it.' I thought I was going to get lynched! I never heard so much booing and hissing in my life. They all wanted Elvis. So the last song on that show is me doing 'Blue Suede Shoes'."

ON HIS WAY OUT THE DOOR, ELVIS MAKES ONE FINAL STOP TO HUG DARLENE FRANKS, DAUGHTER OF HAYRIDE BASS PLAYER AND BOOKING AGENT, TILLMAN FRANKS. TILLMAN, WHO WAS INSTRUMENTAL IN FIRST GETTING ELVIS ON THE HAYRIDE, LOOKS ON FROM BEHIND.

EARLY ON THE MORNING OF **DECEMBER 16, 1956**, ELVIS PACKED HIS BAGS AND LEFT THE CAPTAIN SHREVE HOTEL FOR MEMPHIS, FANS STILL IN TOW.

"ELVIS HAS LEFT THE BUILDING!"

HAYRIDE PROGRAM DIRECTOR AND EMCEE
HORACE LOGAN

The now legendary phrase "Elvis has left the building" was first uttered by Horace Logan that night quite by accident. The show had been a regular performance of the Hayride and Elvis was but the third act of about twenty. Once his performance was over and the encore complete, the crowds of teenagers made for the exits. In a futile plea for the acts that would follow, Horace made the announcement to assure the audience that Elvis would not be back out but that there was still much left of the regular show. The crowd's exodus continued unabated.

"The kids just went berserk," he recalled. "They were running wildly in all directions, trying to position themselves to catch one more glimpse of Elvis, get an autograph, touch him...something. All I know is it was pure pandemonium. Well, sir, I finished my announcements and sat there thinking we've still got a good hour plus to go, so I spoke up to try and regain some order so we could get on with the program."

From the transcripts of that evening, it went like this:

"All right, uh, Elvis has left the building. I have told you absolutely straight up to this point, you know, that he has left the building. He left the stage and went out the back with the policemen and he is now gone from the building.

"I remind you again that the Hayride will continue right on until 11:30 o'clock presenting, again, most of the country artists that you have seen tonight. We'll be very pleased to have you remain with us.

"I invite you also to tune in tonight, all of you who are listening to KWKH, to our Red River Round Up which, beginning at 11:30, will be heard straight through until one o'clock tonight. You'll have the opportunity of hearing on that show a great many of the country music disc jockeys who are visiting with us here tonight in the Youth Building of the Louisiana State Fairgrounds.

"I'd like to remind you that this performance tonight was a benefit performance for the YMCA of the City of Shreveport. Elvis receives no money whatsoever for his performance here tonight. All of the proceeds other than the actual expenses of presenting this show will go to the Shreveport YMCA.

"I must say this for you young ladies and young gentlemen. You have been exactly that: young ladies and young gentlemen, and we are very proud of you for your performance here tonight. It's been so nice having you with us. If you'd like to sit down now, we're going to go on with the show here in just about five minutes. You're listening to the Louisiana Hayride, coming to you from the Youth Building at the Louisiana State Fairgrounds, home for the Centenary College basketball games for 1957."

— Horace Logan

From a lowly beginning in Shreveport, Elvis rose to the heights of world popularity. Norm Bale remembers the 1953 Chevy that Elvis, Scotty Moore, and Bill Black drove to the Hayride on that first night back in October, 1954: "They'd borrowed money to eat dinner before the show."

They were meager times in the beginning but success came fast and in overwhelming amounts. His life would never be the same.

"Elvis would gladly have gone back to East Tupelo," Bill Dugard believes, "to walk that flat dusty path, kick up the dirt, swim in the creek, and shoot the bean shooter. He loved his childhood and never forgot it."

Elvis came back to Shreveport a couple of times after that memorable '56 performance and regularly sent us telegrams updating us on his hectic career. With the medium of television now a permanent fixture and the change in popular music firmly in place, the Louisiana Hayride would fade from sight in the sixties but for Elvis, the journey was just beginning.

Fellow Hayrider Jim Ed Brown recalled the end of an era: "Elvis is the one that all but killed the Hayride because if he was on the Hayride it was a full house. If he was not there, then it wasn't..."

Many groups rush to take credit for Elvis Presley's career but the Louisiana Hayride is not among them. He alone was responsible for creating and maintaining a style that remains unique to this day. Elvis gave rise to Rockabilly which, in turn, became the heart and soul of modern pop music.

Elvis called me on one occasion to urge us to keep the Hayride going and thank us for what we'd done for him. His last appearance in Shreveport was July 1, 1976. On the day he died, I was called by radio and television stations throughout the world to get my reaction... and what do you say?

"The King is dead."

Elvis Presley fan clubs still visit Shreveport and stop by the Municipal Auditorium, which looks the same as it did fifty years ago. They want to stand where he stood, see his dressing room, and see where he lived. Recently, the dressing room was decorated with photos and stories from his Hayride years and the street out front was renamed "Elvis Presley Avenue" in a lasting tribute to this great showman.

In October of 2004, on the 50th anniversary of his fateful arrival in Shreveport, a life size bronze statue of Elvis was dedicated in front of the Auditorium. In August of 2005, another life size bronze of Hayride staff guitarist James Burton, who went on to become a member of the famous TCB band in the late sixties and toured with Elvis the final eight years of his life, was added alongside the statue of the King.

Burton, a native of Shreveport, is one of the all time great musicians. The story goes that the legendary Chet Atkins was once asked what it was like to be the world's greatest living guitarist. His reply? "When did James Burton die?"

Like we were for Hank Williams and the other stars and superstars who walked our stage, the Louisiana Hayride was just a place to pull it all together; a place to rehearse for the big time. But we were also family... and Elvis, the favorite son. Frozen in time are those eighteen months he spent with us, and gone but not forgotten are the teachings of his music and the energy of his performance.

"Uh, well I'd like to say how happy we are to be down here. It's a real honor for us to be... to get a chance to appear on the Louisiana Hayride. We're gonna do a song for ya... You got anything else to say, sir?"
- Elvis Presley

"No, Elvis. Your life and your music said it all."
- Frank Page

(CLOCKWISE FROM TOP LEFT) THE ELVIS STATUE NOW STANDS IN FRONT OF SHREVEPORT'S MUNICIPAL AUDITORIUM; THE JORDANAIRES WERE ON HAND FOR THE DEDICATION OF ELVIS PRESLEY AVENUE; HAYRIDE GUITAR LEGEND JAMES BURTON, THEN AND NOW; AND, FINALLY, FRANK PAGE LOOKS OVER THE ELVIS EXHIBIT AT THE STAGE OF STARS MUSEUM INSIDE THE AUDITORIUM.

PHOTO CREDITS

THANK YOU TO THE FOLLOWING GROUPS OR INDIVIDUALS FOR TAKING AND/OR CONTRIBUTING PHOTOS TO THIS BOOK:

CREDIT(S) READ LEFT TO RIGHT AND FROM TOP TO BOTTOM OF PAGE. ALL COVERS © LOUISIANA HAYRIDE, INC.

JEANELLE ALEXANDER - 19, 98, 99; **LAMAR BAKER** - 13, 59; **JACK BARHAM** - 40, 83, 106, 107, 108, 109, 110, 112, 115, 116, 117, 118, 119, 120, 121, 122, 123, 124, 125, 127, 130, 131, 132, 133, 134, 135, 136, 137, 138, 139, 140, 141, 142, 143, 144, 145, 146, 147, 148, 149, 150, 151, 152, 153, 154, 161, 168; **ERIC BROCK** - 15, 38, 103, 105, 115, 116; **MAXINE BROWN** - 30, 48, 114; **C. G. GRAHAM** - 115, 128, 129; **JUDY HEISERMAN** - 36; **ERNST JORGENSEN** - 21, 33, 42, 44, 48, 52, 53, 57, 69, 70, 71, 73, 74, 76, 78, 80, 81, 82, 89, 90, 91, 92, 96, 105, 158; **LSU-S ARCHIVES** - 40, 81, 159; **TRISH LUTZ** - 11; **CAROL MANGHAM** - 61, 73, 74, 86, 87, 93; **FRANK MCANENY** - 106, 115, 117, 122, 124, 125, 160; **LANGSTON MCEACHERN** - 11, 12, 115; **JOYCE RAILSBACK NICHOLS** - 26, 29, 32, 38, 39, 41, 43, 49, 56, 60; **TOM PACE** - 7, 167; **FRANK PAGE** - 7, 158; **ANN PAULSEN** - 28; **VIRGINIA CLAY PETERSON** - 120; **LOIS ANN RIVERS** - 73, 75, 76, 77, 86, 87, 88, 90, 94; **DIDO ROWLEY** - 37; **RICHARD SOKOLOSKY** - 55; **LLOYD STILLEY** - 115, 162, 163, 164; **NOLAN STRANGE** - 46; **JOHNNY WESSLER** - 7, 167; **LOUISIANA HAYRIDE ARCHIVES** - 8, 14, 15, 16, 17, 18, 19, 20, 21, 22, 23, 24, 25, 26, 28, 29, 30, 31, 32, 33, 34, 35, 39, 40, 41, 42, 43, 44, 45, 46, 47, 48, 50, 51, 53, 54, 55, 56, 57, 58, 59, 60, 61, 62, 64, 65, 66, 68, 72, 73, 78, 79, 81, 83, 84, 85, 89, 91, 94, 95, 96, 97, 98, 99, 100, 102, 103, 105, 114, 120, 123, 130, 132, 155, 156, 157, 158, 160, 165, 167